Moving Beauty

Moving Beauty

THE MONTREAL MUSEUM
OF FINE ARTS

This catalogue was published on the occasion of the exhibition
Moving Beauty, organized by Pierre Théberge, Director,
and presented at the Montreal Museum of Fine Arts
from May 11 to October 15, 1995.

The vehicles were selected by Pierre Théberge, in collaboration with Paul Hunter.
The texts on the automobiles were written by Luc Gagné.

A production of the Publications Service,
Communications Department of the Montreal Museum of Fine Arts
Co-ordination: Denise L. Bissonnette
Translation: Simon Horn, Donald McGrath, Katrin Sermat
Photographic Credits: See list p. 216
Graphic Design and Electronic Publishing: Dufour et Fille Design inc.
Photo-engraving and Printing: Bowne de Montréal inc.

Legal deposit - 2nd quarter 1995
Bibliothèque nationale du Québec
National Library of Canada

ISBN: 2-89192-192-5

Distributed by:
McClelland & Stewart Inc. in Canada
St. Martin's Press in the United States
Fourth Estate Ltd. in the United Kingdom

THE MONTREAL MUSEUM OF FINE ARTS
P.O. Box 3000, Station "H"
Montreal, Quebec H3G 2T9

PRINTED IN CANADA

Contents

Acknowledgements

Our sincerest thanks go first of all to the lenders, who so generously agreed to part with the gems of their collections in order to share them with the public for the duration of our exhibition. Without their enthusiastic co-operation, this project could never have existed.

Many people had a determining influence on the choice of cars selected for this exhibition. The final selection came about through meetings with each one of them, in which they were kind enough to give us the benefit of their advice. To each we owe a substantial debt of friendship and gratitude.

Bernard Lamarre is Honorary President of the Montreal Museum of Fine Arts. It was in his capacity as a member of the Organizing Committee for the XXth World Road Congress that Mr. Lamarre suggested we mount an exhibition on the history of the automobile to coincide with the Congress. He gave us his congenial support throughout the preparations for the exhibition and worked with the private and public sectors to ensure that we had the resources necessary to bring our plans to fruition. For this, we are extremely grateful to him.

Artist and exhibition designer Paul Hunter accompanied us on practically all of our peregrinations to public and private automobile collections throughout the United States and Europe. We had the benefit not only of his consistently pertinent advice, but also of his sharp eye, his sense of humour and his enthusiasm for the scope of the project.

We also gave him the arduous task of deciding how the automobiles would be presented in the galleries, so that visitors to the exhibition could see the important role they have played as sculptures, as objects of art and design. We are certain that he will accomplish this task with panache, and we sincerely thank him for his endeavours.

We wish to thank the Ministère des Transports du Québec and the Société de l'assurance automobile du Québec for their financial assistance, which enabled us to organize the exhibition in conjunction with the XXth World Road Congress, taking place in Montreal from September 3 to 9, 1995. Without their vigorous support, the exhibition could never have been mounted.

Thanks are also due to Luc Gagné, chief editor of the magazine *Le Monde de l'Auto/World of Wheels*, who agreed to write the catalogue entries documenting the automobiles we selected. We are fortunate that we could rely on his comprehensive knowledge of the history of the automobile.

Other individuals were also generous with their advice, and our sincerest thanks go out to them as well:

Antonio Amadelli
Musée Biscaretti de l'automobile,
Turin

Hubert Auran
Noves, France

Diane Bélair
Montreal International Auto Show

André Binda
Nice

Klaus Bischof
Porsche-Museum, Stuttgart

Robert J. Boudeman
Richland, Michigan

Lloyd Buck
Arturo Keller Collection,
Petaluma, California

Gilbert Bureau
Montreal

Robert H. Casey
Henry Ford Museum & Greenfield
Village, Dearborn, Michigan

Chris Charlton
Robert Bahre
Oxford, Maine

Phil J. Chartrand
Montreal

Nicolangelo Cioppi
Groupe automobile Silver Star,
Greenfield Park, Quebec

Jean-Claude Delerm
Anne Marcuzzi
Musée national de l'Automobile de
Mulhouse, France

Yves Desgrees du Lou
La Colline de l'automobile, Paris

Jean-Denys Devauges
Musée national de la Voiture et du
Tourisme, Compiègne, France

C. Fock
HET Nationaal Automobiel-
Museum, Raamsdonksveer,
Netherlands

Jackie L. Frady
National Automobile Museum,
Reno, Nevada

Léonard Gianadda
Fondation Pierre Gianadda,
Martigny, Switzerland

Gilles Godbout
Harold Tremblay
Direction des Communications,
Ministère des Transports du
Québec

Margaret Goldsmith
Indianapolis

Hugo Gravel
Infiniti Laval, Laval, Quebec

Richard Grenon
Sainte-Anne-de-Bellevue, Quebec

Jim Hall
Chaparral Cars, Midland, Texas

David Holls
Detroit

Christina Hunter
Max Hunter
New York

Mark W. Hutchins
Ford Motor Company of Canada Ltd,
Oakville, Ontario

Paul and Barbara Karassik
Saint Petersburg, Florida

Peter Kaus
Rosso Bianco Collection,
Aschaffenburg, Germany

Jean-Louis Laine
Musée Peugeot, Sochaux, France

Michael Lamm
Stockton, California

G. Y. Landry
Chrysler Canada Ltd, Windsor

Robert de Lano Sutherland
Englewood, Colorado

Yvon Lebeau
Société de l'assurance automobile
du Québec

Charles Lemaître
Hardwick, Massachusetts

Kent Liffick
Indianapolis Motor Speedway Hall
of Fame Museum, Indianapolis

Gian Luigi Longinotti Buitoni
Michael B. Jackling
Paolo Letta
Ferrari North America Inc.,
Englewood Cliffs, New Jersey

Adrien Maeght
Galerie Adrien Maeght, Paris

Antonio Magro
Museo Storico Alfa-Romeo,
Arese, Italy

Frank Marketti
Behring Automobile Museum,
Danville, California

Norbert Michel
Musée de l'automobiliste,
Mougins, France

Philipp Moch
Chavignon, France

Hans Neuendorf
Frankfurt

Marc Nicolosi
François Melcion
Rétromobile, Paris

Daniel Noiseux
Montreal

George A. Peapples
General Motors of Canada,
Oshawa, Ontario

Paolo Pininfarina
Fredi Valentini
Silvana Appendino
Pininfarina, Turin

Walter Rathjen
Deutsches Museum, Munich

Mr. and Mrs. Charles Renaud
Basel

Federico Robutti
Stefano Benetti Genolini
Quattroruote Collection, Milan

Charles Roy
Montreal

Paul Russell
Essex, Massachusetts

Robert Sbarge
Matthew S. Short
Gregg Buttermore
Auburn-Cord-Duesenberg Museum,
Auburn, Indiana

Anneliese Schillinger
Christopher E. Bangle
BMW Museum, Munich

Joseph F. Sexton
Indianapolis

Hagan Stewart
Imperial Palace Auto Collection,
Las Vegas

Eric Touchette
Bibliauto, Montreal

Bernard Vaireaux
Musée Henri Malartre, Lyons

Jacques Vaucher
L'art et l'automobile, New York

Mario Verdun di Cantogno
Centro Storico Fiat, Turin

H. von Pein
Dieter Ritter
Georg Auffarth
Mercedes-Benz-Museum, Stuttgart

Michael E. Ware
National Motor Museum Beaulieu,
England

Count Jacques R. de
Wurstenberger
René Rey
Gilly, Switzerland

    An exhibition of this scope would not have been possible without the financial support of numerous private companies and government organizations. Among our sponsors, we wish first of all to thank Mercedes-Benz Canada Inc., as well as Imperial Oil Ltd., Reynolds Aluminum Company of Canada, Air France, Hydro-Québec, Michelin North America (Canada) Inc. and Pepsi-Cola Canada Beverages. *La Presse* and the magazine *Le monde de l'Auto/World of Wheels* contributed promotional support for the exhibition. Insurance costs were provided by the Department of Canadian Heritage through its Insurance Program for Travelling Exhibitions. As well, the generous contribution of the Ministère du Tourisme du Québec enabled us to undertake greater efforts to draw tourists to the show.

We are also grateful to those at the Ministère des Transports and the Société de l'Assurance automobile du Québec who worked closely with our Educational and Cultural Service and our Travelling Exhibition Service in preparing the educational component of the exhibition, which is devoted to road safety and the highway code.

The Ministère de la Culture et des Communications du Québec and the Conseil des arts de la Communauté urbaine de Montréal are also deserving of credit. Their annual grant programmes enable the Museum to function and give it the means to organize major exhibitions.

The members of the Museum's Board of Trustees and the Programming Advisory Committee are entitled to our deepest gratitude for their unconditional support of this project.

Finally, we wish to thank all those at the Montreal Museum of Fine Arts who in any way contributed to the organization of this exhibition. Their devotion, competence and acute sense of responsibility made this exhibition possible.

Pierre Théberge, C.Q.
Director
The Montreal Museum of Fine Arts

List of lenders

The Montreal Museum of Fine Arts wishes to thank the following lenders to the exhibition:

Centro Storico Fiat, Turin
Walter Baran Collection, Ashland, Pennsylvania
Boudeman Collection, Richland, Michigan
Phil J. Chartrand Collection
Château de Vincy Collection, Switzerland
Arturo Keller Collection, Petaluma, California
Ralph Lauren Collection
Philipp Moch Collection
Rosso Bianco Collection, Aschaffenburg, Germany
Deutsches Museum, Munich
Ferrari North America Inc., Englewood Cliffs, New Jersey
Ferrari SpA Maranello, Italy
Richard Grenon, Au-Temps-Tic Auto, Sainte-Anne-de-Bellevue, Quebec
The William F. Harrah Foundation National Automobile Museum, Reno, Nevada
Indianapolis Motor Speedway Hall of Fame Museum, Indianapolis
Barbara and Paul Karassik
Lions Club International, District 103, Île-de-France Est
Mercedes-Benz-Museum, Stuttgart
Musée Henri-Malartre, Lyons, France
Musée national de l'Automobile de Mulhouse, France, Schlumpf Collection
Musée national de la Voiture et du Tourisme, Compiègne, France
Museo Storico Alfa-Romeo, Arese, Italy
Pininfarina
Porsche-Museum, Stuttgart-Zuffenhausen, Germany

as well as those who prefer to remain anonymous.

Introduction

PIERRE THÉBERGE

THE AUTOMOBILE, AN OBJECT OF ART AND DESIGN AND A PRODUCT OF THE imagination and creativity of inventors, builders, engineers and designers around the world. It was this machine that inspired the present exhibition, *Moving Beauty*.

During our visits to major public and private collections in Great Britain, Holland, France, Belgium, Switzerland, Germany, Italy, Canada and the United States, we had the opportunity to witness firsthand the remarkable variety of forms the automobile has assumed since its relatively brief history began in 1886. Each automobile in this exhibition somehow reflected the spirit of its age, yet, in the mind of its creator, it also embodied the ideal vehicle. And this ideal vehicle, as exemplified by some of its most splendid specimens, is what we want to show you here.

Our research has revealed that, from its inception, the automobile has conformed to two basic morphological types. The first, which was perhaps the easier one to design and build, resulted from the transformation of the horse-drawn carriage into a self-propelled vehicle, that is, one that owes its motion to an independent gasoline, steam or electric engine rather than to a horse. The vast majority of automobiles are variations on this first type.

The second type, which inspired this exhibition, appeared around the same time as the first. It owes its existence to the perseverance of certain individuals who, like Leonardo da Vinci[1] and Nicolas-Joseph Cugnot[2] (1725-1804), invented a new vehicle totally removed from the tradition of the horseless carriage. Most of the cars you will see in this exhibition exemplify this truly revolutionary, experimental and prototypical automobile. The same holds for that section of the show which is devoted to the automobile of tomorrow, since this is, by definition, the ideal vehicle.

The physical constraints of our exhibition space make it impossible to do justice to a subject as broad as the automobile. We therefore excluded certain aspects of its history, such as its technical development (as fascinating as this may be), its role in urban civilization and its influence upon the development of society.

We are also aware that modern artists very quickly appreciated the importance of the automobile as a revolutionary instrument ideally suited for overturning secular cultural traditions. This idea was forcefully expressed by Marinetti in his "Futurist Manifesto" of 1909: "We say that the splendour of the world has been enriched

1   On Leonardo's "self-propelling wagon", see Augusto Marinoni, "Leonardo's Impossible Machines", in *Leonardo da Vinci: Engineer and Architect*, exhib. cat. (Montreal: Montreal Museum of Fine Arts, 1987) pp. 124-125.

2   The "fardier", powered by a steam engine invented by Cugnot in 1771, is part of the collection of the Conservatoire des Arts et Métiers in Paris.

with a new beauty, the beauty of speed. A racing car whose hood is adorned with great pipes like serpents of explosive breath – a roaring car that seems to run on grapeshot – is more beautiful than the *Victory of Samothrace*."[3]

Many of these artists integrated visual elements from the world of the automobile into their works. Several among them, including Francis Picabia, Georges Braque, Pablo Picasso and Fernand Léger, were unabashedly delighted to own fine cars, while others, such as Sonia Delaunay, Le Corbusier and Marcel Breuer, were happy to design automobiles for various manufacturers.

Although an excellent theme in itself, the relationship between art and the automobile is not covered here because it was already explored in the 1984 exhibition *Automobile and Culture* at the Los Angeles Museum of Contemporary Art.[4] Nor did we delve into the broader question of the links between twentieth-century art and the machine, since this was the subject of the New York Museum of Modern Art's 1968 exhibition, *The Machine as Seen at the End of the Mechanical Age*.[5]

Finally, we left out yet another fascinating theme: the automobile and film, two contemporary inventions whose paths have crossed. Starting with Georges Méliès, the automobile rapidly became a movie star[6] and even spawned a clearly defined genre – the "road movie". Last summer the Cinémathèque québécoise screened a series of such films, in the process exhibiting its characteristic sensitivity and enthusiasm.[7]

What was left to explore, you may ask? Simply the dream offered to us by these masterpieces in motion, these examples of the "ideal vehicle" magnificently displayed in the superb galleries of the Museum. Here is an exhibition that is perfectly in tune with the spirit of the Museum, which has always displayed an interest in all manifestations of the visual arts.

To illustrate the invention of the modern automobile, we chose the very first patented vehicle propelled by an internal combustion engine, the 1886 Benz (cat. 1). With its borrowings from the tricycle, the meticulously constructed Benz bears witness to the birth of automobile design. The aristocratic elegance of the car, its jaunty air verging on exuberance, make it one of the finest examples of the early automobile.

Aerodynamic design makes its first appearance in the history of the automobile with *La Jamais-Contente* (cat. 2) produced in 1899 by Belgian engineer Camille Jenatzy.[8]

This vehicle was designed to break speed records. Shaped like a torpedo and devoid of exterior ornamentation (headlights, mudguards, windshield, etc.), *La Jamais-Contente* was radically different from its contemporaries and could cut through the air with much less resistance. It was a prototype (only one was ever built)

3   *Marinetti: Selected Writings*, ed. R. W. Flint, trans. R. W. Flint and Arthur A. Coppotelli (New York: Farrar, Straus and Giroux, 1971).

4   Gerald Silk, "The Automobile as Art", in *Automobile and Culture*, exhib. cat. (Los Angeles: Los Angeles Museum of Contemporary Art, 1984) pp. 25-169. See also Reimar Zeller, ed., *Das Automobil in der Kunst, 1886-1986* (Munich: Prestel, 1986); D. B. Tubbs, *Art and the Automobile* (Secaucus, N. J.: Charwell Books, 1989); *La vitesse*, exhib. cat. (Paris: Fondation Cartier/Flammarion, 1991).

5   K. G. Pontus Hulten, *The Machine as Seen at the End of the Mechanical Age*, exhib. cat. (New York: The Museum of Modern Art, 1968).

6   Kerry Brougher, "The Car as Star", in *Automobile and Culture*, 1984, pp. 171-174.

7   Robert Daudelin, "Road Movies", *La Revue de la Cinémathèque*, July-August 1994, and the schedule of screenings, Cinémathèque québécoise, Montreal.

8   See G. Howard, *Aérodynamique Automobile* (Paris: Éditions Presse Audiovisuel E.P.A., 1988). See Franz Engler and Claude Lichtenstein, *The Esthetics of Minimized Drag Streamlined, A Metaphor for Progress* (Baden, Switzerland: Lars Müller).

and its sole objective was speed. These characteristics make it the direct ancestor of all racing cars, right up to today's Formula 1 racers.

The 1914 Alfa 40/60 Ricotti (coachwork by Castagna (cat. 3) was commissioned by Count Ricotti. As revolutionary as *La Jamais-Contente*, it was, however, meant for town and country driving rather than the race course. Its ovoid body was clearly intended to meet aerodynamic requirements, and it was one of the first automobiles to come equipped with an all-enveloping metal body. Like something straight out of a Jules Verne novel, this car, with its "Liberty" styling, anticipated the variations on the circle, oval and curved line that would appear in Europe and the United States in the 1930s. This trend is eloquently illustrated by several of the vehicles in the exhibition.

The 1916 Miller Golden Submarine (cat. 4) was a contemporary of the Alfa Ricotti. The passenger compartment of the American car exemplified the same aerodynamic principles as its Italian counterpart, but its motor housing remained that of the race car it really was. The car was designed by Harry Miller; one of the most original American inventors of his time, he would later create a masterpiece among racing cars, the 1928 Miller 91 (cat. 8).

Two other great automotive pioneers, France's Gabriel Voisin and Germany's Edmund Rumpler, took experience acquired building airplanes during World War I and applied it to the construction of automobiles that were totally new for their time.

The 1921 Rumpler *Tropfenwagen* 0A 104 [teardrop-shaped vehicle] (cat. 5) was designed for city driving and expounded a totally new vision of aerodynamic design. The overall appearance of the car recalls the gondola of the dirigibles of the same period. The *Tropfenwagen* had more in common with the Alfa 40/60 Ricotti, the Miller Golden Submarine and *La Jamais-Contente* than with its contemporaries, whose rectangular shapes, straight lines and right angles dominated the world over. In the United States, for example, there was the ubiquitous Ford Model T, while Europe had the Rolls-Royce, the Mercedes-Benz and the Lancia.

Racing cars and passenger automobiles are exhibited side by side in this exhibition, since they have, after all, developed in tandem, with racing vehicles acting as stylistic and technical laboratories for their more utilitarian cousins.

The 1923 Voisin *C6 Laboratoire* (cat. 6) was an ultralight aluminum racing machine, low to the ground and clearly inspired by the shape of an aircraft wing. Like *La Jamais-Contente*, it was built solely to win races and had no accessories to slow it down.

The elegance and lightness of the 1928 Miller 91 (cat. 8) contrasts with the mass and obvious power of the 1926 Panhard-Levassor 35cv (cat. 7). Although both were designed to break speed records, their builders adopted different forms and techniques in the attempt to reach the same goal. The shape of the Panhard-Levassor fit naturally into the growing tradition of the large racing car; its designers saw the vehicle's weight and its powerful engine as the keys to victory. Whereas the Voisin C6 *Laboratoire* had angular, even cubist lines, the Panhard-Levassor displayed a series of curves that are more characteristic of the racing car of the 1930s (see cat. 13, 20, 23) than that of the early 1920s.

Around the 1930s, luxury sports cars began to make their appearance in both Europe and the United States. Their elegant, luxurious coachwork aptly expressed the exuberance of the age. An American car such as the 1929 Auburn 8-120 Boattail (cat. 9) is a classic example of this trend.

This luxury vehicle may be compared to the 1931-1932 Mercedes-Benz SSK Trossi (cat. 11). Of German origin, with British coachwork designed for an Italian buyer, the Trossi was almost surrealist with its bat's-wing rear and its unusual proportions. As we can see from its Art nouveau curves and arabesques[9], the car exhibited all the characteristics of the European high style that flourished during the period. It is more evocative of the Picasso of the Marie-Thérèse period than of the Fernand Léger of the *Mécanicien*.[10]

The 1930 Alfa-Romeo 6C 1750 *Gran Sport* (cat. 10) was designed to be a racing car and a sports car all in one. In many respects the first modern sports car, its light design (created by the Italian coachbuilder Zagato) would have enormous influence on the evolution of form right up to the present. The 1938 BMW 328 (cat. 22) built a few years later, echoed the form of the Alfa-Romeo but was more fluidly aerodynamic.

Record-breakers owe their existence solely to the determination of their inventors, builders and drivers to create vehicles capable of smashing every previous record. The 1978 Mercedes-Benz C-111/III (cat. 42) is a magnificent example of this breed.

Like *La Jamais-Contente*, this vehicle had a body designed to provide the least possible air resistance and an engine whose sole purpose was to break all world speed records. While this represented, perhaps, a search for the ideal, it has long been known that the faster an automobile goes the more likely it is to leave the road entirely, with all the tragic consequences this entails. It was therefore necessary, in both cases, to stabilize steering with the aid of a rear fin and to come up with an all-enveloping body as low to the ground as possible so that the downward air pressure would keep the wheels on the road. Never before have form and function been so tightly interwoven as in these two ephemeral vehicles.

The 1930s saw the emergence of a new style of racing car with a more rounded profile that took account of new developments in

9 Jean-Paul Bouillon gives a brilliant analysis of the arabesque in late nineteenth-century European art in his essay "Arabesques", in *Lost Paradise: Symbolist Europe*, exhib. cat. (Montreal: Montreal Museum of Fine Arts, 1995) pp. 376-384. Even automobile design in the 1930s was affected by the phenomenon, albeit later in time.

10 Ferdinand Léger, *The Mechanic*, 1920. Ottawa, National Gallery of Canada.

aerodynamic design. The 1934 Alfa-Romeo B *Aerodinamica* (cat.13), the 1938-1939 Bowes Seal Fast Special (cat. 23), the 1938 Auto-Union D V12 (cat. 20) and even the 1947 Cisitalia-Porsche 360 Grand Prix (cat. 33) are all exceptional illustrations of formal elegance.

It was also during the 1930s that stylistic and technical research made the greatest strides, especially in style and aerodynamic design. The 1934 Chrysler Airflow (cat. 14) and the 1947 Tatra 87 (cat. 19) represent purely technical solutions, shaped by a development program whose goals were more technical than stylistic. At both Chrysler and Tatra, with its 1933-1934 Tatra 77, the search for mechanical perfection and the ultimate in aerodynamic design almost compelled the body designers of these two automobiles to favour function over "style."

Other builders took a somewhat less radical approach, creating vehicles with stylistically lighter, more visually appealing bodies.

The 1935 Voisin C25 *Aérodyne* (cat. 15) and the 1937 Panhard-Levassor Dynamic 130 X 76 (cat. 17), with their refined form and dynamic appearance seem inspired by Art Deco aesthetics. Gordon Buehrig's 1936 Cord 810 Westchester (cat. 18), all circles and ovals, provided a worthy rival to the greatest European creations of the day. Of all the historic vehicles in this exhibition, the Cord is the one that most strongly influenced contemporary automotive design.

The slanting windshield and flaring fins of the 1933 Bugatti 46 Coach *Profilé* (cat. 12) give it the appearance of a grasshopper. At rest, the car conveys an impression of lightness and speed. The 1938 Bugatti 57 Atlantic (cat. 24) is a designer's dream. With its low body and its prominent, almost skull-like passenger compartment, the Atlantic is, perhaps, the one that most closely approaches the ideal of absolute perfection in automobile design. Finally, we have the 1939 Bugatti 64 Coach (cat. 27); this last brainchild of Jean Bugatti, who died the year it was built, anticipated a number of developments in automotive aesthetics.

We shall also see three other automobiles that exemplify innovative solutions to the era's problems of form. The 1938 Talbot Lago T 150 SS (cat. 26), produced in the workshops of Figoni and Falaschi, is similar in shape and size to the Bugatti 57 Atlantic, but seems less technically oriented and more traditional. Influenced by Art Deco and biomorphism, it is the epitome of refinement, a witness to French aesthetics of the period. Like the 1938 Bentley 4 1/4 L Embiricos (cat. 21), it was one of the last products of the dazzling imagination of French manufacturers and coachbuilders between the wars.

The 1939 Lagonda Le Mans Lancefield V12 (cat. 28) and the 1939 Mercedes-Benz 320 (cat. 29) adopted aerodynamic elegance in styling, while retaining certain traditional forms of the 1920s, especially in the front. The 1936 Lancia Astura Pinin Farina (cat. 16) was distinguished from its contemporaries by its prophetic horizontal lines and its elongated appearance. Its classic lines and subdued shape heralded the post-war evolution of Italian design, which would have considerable influence around the world right up to the present.

Following the enforced halt to automobile production imposed by World War II, the 1940s would see new stylistic experiments on both sides of the Atlantic.

The Hollywood styling of the 1940 Chrysler Newport Dual Cowl Phaeton (cat. 30) seems to combine both the streamlined tradition of the 1930s and the enveloping coachwork that would characterize American automobiles of the late 1940s.

The technological and stylistic innovations of the 1948 Tucker (cat. 35) provided a totally original version of the American family car. This vehicle placed form at the service of technological progress, a trend also exemplified by the 1934 Chrysler Airflow CU and the Tatra 87. In its own way, the Tucker was a "show car," like the "dream cars" and "concept cars" that were built for advertising purposes and that would have such an impact on the auto show circuit in both North America and Europe.

Like the Tucker, André Dubonnet's exclusive 1938-1946 Dubonnet Xenia (cat. 25) was influenced by the most recent developments in jet aircraft. This French product adopted a style midway between the Mercedes-Benz Trossi and the 1938 Talbot Lago. With the 1949 Bentley Mark VI Pinin Farina (cat. 36), Pinin Farina managed to create a light and refined body for a car which, in other hands, would have shown rather heavy lines.

Finally, the simplicity of the 1947 Fiat 1100S 50 (cat. 32) reminds us that the aerodynamic elegance of post-war Italian design would inspire many car builders around the world.

In 1947, Ferrari built its first automobile, the Ferrari 125S (cat. 31), launching a line that would take on almost mythic proportions among both connoisseurs and the general public. In Germany, Ferdinand Porsche launched the 1948 Porsche 356 No. 1 (cat. 34), a revolutionary vehicle whose broad, low body would serve as the model for sports and racing cars in the postwar period. Later automobiles would adhere ever more closely to the horizontal plane of the road.

The light and fanciful appearance of the 1952 Alfa-Romeo 1900 *Disco volante* (cat. 37) would also have a great influence on foreign automobile designers, including the *Jaguar* team. Mercedes-Benz continued its explorations of style with its 1954 W 196 *Stromlinienwagen* (cat. 38), which brought the automobile's form into line with the horizontal plane of the road. The curving lines of the 1955 Jaguar D (cat. 39) suggested other ways of reconciling performance with form. It made use of the rear fin, a feature already seen on the 1934 Alfa-Romeo B *Aerodinamica* (cat. 13).

The great racing cars of the last three decades are represented by four vehicles, each a solution to the problem of reconciling ever-increasing speed with the equally important requirement of keeping the wheels on the road. The 1979 Chaparral-Cosworth 2K (cat. 43) was equipped with a horizontal rear spoiler, a feature already used on Jim Hall's 1966 Chaparral 2E. (The Chaparral 2E's spoiler was, however, adjustable.) This approach would be also be taken by other builders, as we see from the 1977 Porsche 936/77 Spyder (cat. 41) and the 1987 Ferrari F1/87 (cat. 44).

The 1957 Cadillac 57-70 Eldorado Brougham (cat. 40) is a magnificent illustration of the desire of 1950s American car makers to create vehicles that epitomized the "American Dream" and the society of abundance it represented. A perfunctory comparison of the Eldorado with the Fiat 1100 or the Alfa-Romeo *Disco volante* reveals the enormous cultural differences between Americans and Europeans, differences that were evident in their varying styles of automotive design.

Our timeline for the exhibition stops with the Eldorado, for a very good reason. In the 1960s, the automobile entered a new era that completely changed both its appearance and its function. In North America in particular, the link between the car and the consumer society's dream of abundance and prosperity would be abruptly severed. The automobile has gradually become more of a utilitarian vehicle, required above all to respect increasingly strict safety and environmental regulations. Today, racing cars are the only exception to this general rule.

Today's public is aware of the crucial importance of protecting the environment, and this concern has led auto-makers around the world to conceive of the automobile's future in a totally different fashion.

For an idea of the automobile of the future, we asked the Pininfarina company to present three vehicles developed as part of their Ethos line (cat. 46, 47, 48). From its inception, this firm, represented in our exhibition by two historic vehicles, the Lancia Astura (cat. 16) and the Bentley Mark VI (cat. 36), has continued to create particularly reflined bodies for high-performance vehicles. The Mythos (cat. 45) is a prototype that was developed for the chassis and engine of a powerful Ferrari in 1989. The Ethos project marked a new step forward for the company. These cars combine innovative styling with technologies that effectively meet the most stringent environmental standards.

The final portion of our exhibition concerns safety and road signs, and is presented as part of our educational activities.

We hope that visitors to this exhibition have been able to rediscover all the beauty and magic of the automobile, and to appreciate the artistic ideals and lyric dreams that spurred its creators.

Catalogue

1.

Benz 1886

KARL BENZ WAS A DEVOTEE OF THE VELOCIPEDE. IT WAS DURING A particularly exhausting ride in the 1860s that he first entertained the idea of fitting such a vehicle with a light gas-powered engine. The engine, he thought, would replace muscle-power and make people more mobile.

A decade went by before Benz actually began to develop the engine. He was, in fact, betting on this project to ensure the survival of the engine manufacturing company he had founded during an economic recession.

Benz had to overcome a major obstacle at the outset. In 1877, another German, Nikolaus August Otto,[1] had obtained a patent for the principle of the 4-stroke liquid-fuel engine. Rather than pay Otto for a license, Benz was forced to work on a 2-stroke design. It took him three long years to develop his 2-cylinder engine, which was finally operational on New Year's Eve, 1879. The design of the engine, which featured an electric ignition, was unprecedented. Benz was unable to patent it, however, and the engine did not provide enough thrust to propel a vehicle. Benz nonetheless found a market for it in the industrial sector, thus generating sorely needed income for his business.

In 1884, Benz began developing a new, 4-stroke engine. He was counting on Otto losing a legal dispute with other manufacturers whom Otto had accused of stealing "his" invention.

At the beginning of 1886, Benz's single-cylinder engine was ready for use in a vehicle. It was mounted over the rear wheels on a chassis of welded steel tubing, with its piston and flywheel set in a horizontal position. Benz feared that setting the enormous flywheel vertically might produce a gyroscopic effect that would interfere with the vehicle's steering.

The spoked wheels and solid rubber tires were derived from bicycle equipment (Benz manufactured bicycle spokes). The front wheel was set in a fork that was also similar to the fork on a bicycle.

Karl Benz had hoped to build a four-wheeled vehicle, but had difficulty devising an effective steering system. Instead, he opted for

Benz 1886

ENGINE
Type: single-cylinder, single carburetor (later a single constant-level heated carburetor) Displacement: 985 cc. Bore and stroke: 91.4 mm x 150 mm. Horsepower: 0.885 hp at 400 rpm

DIMENSIONS
Length: 2,600 mm; width: 1,450 mm; height: 1,500 mm; wheelbase: not provided; weight: 263 kg

TRANSMISSION
Direct with clutch mechanism

PERFORMANCE
Maximum speed: 15 km/h

COLLECTION
Mercedes-Benz-Museum, Stuttgart

1   Ickx 1971, p. 126.

a single, pivoting front wheel, its rack and pinion steering operated by a tiller.

Power from the engine was transmitted directly, through a clutch mechanism, to a drive belt attached to a transverse countershaft. Each end of the shaft was fitted with a cogwheel and chain, which in turn powered the rear wheels. There was no reverse gear.

On January 29, 1886, the Berlin Imperial Patent Office granted Karl Benz patent number 37,435 for his "gas engine-propelled vehicle".[2] The patent made no mention of the automobile's 4-stroke engine but, coincidentally, a court decision voided Otto's patent the following day.

The car's first trial run was marred by an accident; Benz lost control and hit the wall surrounding his small factory. During the vehicle's first public showing, on June 28, 1886, it went barely 100 yards.[3] Before the year was out, however, Karl Benz had succeeded in travelling a distance of 10 km.

2   In "L'invention capitale de Karl Benz", p. 5, Daimler Benz AG press release.

3   Ickx 1971, p. 138.

Benz was also the first motorist to receive a registration for an automobile. It was issued by the Baden authorities on August 1, 1888. That same month,[4] Karl Benz's wife Berta, accompanied by her two young sons, is said to have ushered in the era of motorcar touring when she drove 80 km from Mannheim to Pforzheim[5] to visit her mother, without her husband's knowledge. She set off on this journey to inspire him and to persuade him to put his automobile on public display. A month later, Benz was awarded a gold medal for the automobile at the Munich Industrial Exhibition.

The Benz Tricycle was the first automobile sold to the general public. Some fifteen of the tricycles were manufactured between 1888 and 1893.[6]

4   Ward 1974, Vol. 2, p. 173.

5   Mercedes-Benz/Kimes 1986, p. 42.

6   Porázik 1981, p. 50.

2.

La Jamais-Contente 1899

It is the turn of the century. A Belgian challenges a French count. The duelists' weapon of choice: the automobile. At stake: the title of fastest man on earth.

The story began when Paul Meyan, founder of the *Automobile Club de France* and publisher of *La France Automobile* magazine, announced that a hill-climb contest would be held at Chanteloup near Paris on November 26, 1898. Among the contestants was the Belgian Camille Jenatzy, an engineer for the *Compagnie internationale des transports automobiles* (CITA) in Paris. Driving an electric dogcart built by his own firm, he ascended the hill in 3 minutes, 52 seconds[1] at an average speed of 27 km/h[2] and won the contest.

Surprised by the interest the contest generated, Paul Meyan announced on December 10 that a 2-km race would be held. It should be remembered that the average speed of automobiles of the time was about 25 km/h. On December 18, Count Gaston de Chasseloup-Laubat set a record on the main avenue of the Achères agricultural park, reaching 63.144 km/h[3] with a 40-hp electric Janteaud.

Jenatzy had been unable to compete, but the following day he wrote to Meyan, challenging anyone to top his speed. He went so far as to stake five hundred gold francs[4] on the outcome of this automotive duel. Chasseloup-Laubat took up the challenge.

The contest got under way on January 17, 1899. Camille Jenatzy went first, driving the dogcart[5] he had used the previous year. He broke the Frenchman's record, reaching 66.664 km/h. His rival then set a new standard at 70.585 km/h.[6] The competition continued to escalate. On January 27, Jenatzy covered the 2-km course in 1 minute, 41 4/5 seconds, reaching a speed of 79.995 km/h. Then, on March 4, Chasseloup-Laubat set a new record of 92.307 km/h, driving a more-streamlined Janteaud.

Jenatzy also believed in the virtues of streamlining. CITA was already working on a new, cigar-shaped electric car that Jenatzy baptized in his own image as *La Jamais-Contente* [Never Satisfied].

La Jamais-Contente 1899

ENGINE
Type: two Postel-Vinay electric motors. Fueled by Fulmen storage batteries.[7]
Horsepower: 67 hp

DIMENSIONS
Length: 3,600 mm; width: 1,580 mm; height: 1,350 mm; wheelbase: 1,840 mm; weight: 1,000 kg[8]

TRANSMISSION
Direct drive motors, one on each rear wheel Connected in series or parallel, providing the equivalent of 6 speeds[9]

PERFORMANCE
Maximum speed: 106 km/h

COLLECTION
Musée national de la Voiture et du Tourisme, Compiègne, France

1   *Jamais-Contente*/Leman 1984, p. 34.

2   Ward 1974, p. 1,091.

3   *Jamais-Contente*/Leman 1984, p. 35.

4   *Jamais-Contente*/Tavard n. d., p. 6.

5   Ibid, p. 9.

6   *Jamais-Contente*/Leman 1984, p. 35.

7   Casucci 1981, p.213.

8   Rousseau and Caron 1993, entry 187.

9   Casucci 1981, p. 213.

Original

The vehicle was mounted on a conventional chassis with four semi-elliptical leaf springs, and a transversal leaf spring connected to the steering system. The wheels were fitted with solid Michelin tires. The body, designed by Léon Aucher at the Rothschild coachbuilders in Paris, was made of partinium, a primitive aluminum alloy invented by Frenchman Henri Partin. Partinium was used to lighten the vehicle; half of its 1500-kg weight came from the rechargeable batteries.

On March 31, Jenatzy unveiled his secret weapon at Achères but only reached a speed of 83.903 km/h. A month later, on April 29, 1899, the road still damp from the morning mist, Jenatzy surged forward at the helm of his four-wheeled cigar. He struggled to maintain control of the double handlebars mounted on the vertical steering column. By the end of the contest, he had broken the 100 km/h barrier, covering 1 km in 34 seconds at a speed of 105.879 km/h.[10] At 31 years of age, he had become "the fastest man in the world." Following this exploit, Jenatzy and Chasseloup-Laubat put an end to their duel.

10 *Jamais-Contente*/Leman 1984, p. 35.

Replica

Some would attempt to minimize the achievement, remarking that *La Jamais-Contente* had been designed specifically to break the speed record. It is also worth mentioning that in England in 1835, 64 years earlier, a Sharp and Roberts steam locomotive had reached a speed of 101.53 km/h, or 25 leagues per hour.[11]

Almost a century later, on April 16, 1994, a faithful replica of *La Jamais-Contente* was unveiled in France. It represents the culmination of two years' work by students at the Mireille-Grenet technical high school in Compiègne. The project was supervised by Joël Debout, professor of mechanical engineering at the Université de technologie de Compiègne (UTC) and was made possible with financial support from the local Lions' Club. Unlike its ancestor displayed at the Musée national de la voiture et du tourisme de Compiègne, which no longer has its engine, battery or even its original tires, the replica is in running condition. It sports grey Michelin tires identical to the originals and batteries provided by Fulmen. It is even equipped with a cigar-shaped body made of modern sheet aluminum supplied by the French aluminum producer Péchiney. Unfortunately, the formula for manufacturing partinium has been lost over the years.

11 *Jamais-Contente*/Tavard, p. 3.

La Jamais-Contente at the Tuileries
flower festival on June 12, 1899.
The woman with the parasol is
Mme Jenatzy.

Photo: Hutin, Compiègne

La *Jamais-Contente* in action during
its final attempt to break a record
(105 km/h) on April 29, 1899.

3.

Alfa 40/60 Ricotti 1914

Alfa 40/60 Ricotti 1914

ENGINE
Type: in-line 4-cylinder. Displacement: 6,082 cc.
Bore and stroke: 110 mm x 160 mm. Horsepower: 70 hp at 2,200 rpm[1]

DIMENSIONS
Length: 5,350 mm; width: 1,660 mm; height: 2,230 mm;
wheelbase: 3,220 mm; weight: 1,000 kg

TRANSMISSION
4-speed manual

PERFORMANCE
Maximum speed: 139 km/h

COLLECTION
Museo Storico Alfa-Romeo, Arese, Italy

COUNT MARCO RICOTTI WANTED TO MAKE A STATEMENT. LIKE FELLOW Italians Prince Scipion Borghese and Count Giovanni Lurani, he was driven by a desire to own the fastest and most impressive automobile of his time.

He therefore asked Milanese coachbuilder Ercole Castagna to produce the most exceptional bodywork ever fitted to the chassis of an Alfa 40/60. Since the car had to be the fastest as well as the most impressive, streamlining was obviously essential. Thus was born the *Aerodinamica*.

The body – you could almost call it the cabin – made one think of airplanes, or even dirigibles. Made of riveted aluminium sheeting, it had portholes for windows and small horizontal wings instead of the traditional rounded mudguards. Even the windshield – which in those days usually consisted of one or two rectangular sheets of flat glass – had been replaced by three convex sections, two of which wrapped around the sides of the body. The body's rear section tapered to a point, like a zeppelin.

Like the cab of a modern heavy truck, which literally envelops the engine, the body of Castagna's aerodynamic machine extended forward over the engine, thus completely eliminating the front end overhang. Also, since the chassis had not been modified, Castagna included an air intake for the radiator, which was set about 50 cm into the body.

Since Castagna had merely covered the Alfa's chassis, passengers could actually see the original hood.

In 1915, Count Ricotti literally "converted" his automobile into a open-top model. The top section of the body, from the steering wheel to the rear seat, was cut away and removed, probably to improve ventilation of the passenger compartment. This transformation completely negated the originality of Castagna's design.

Between the wars, however, the body was restored according to the original design. This explains why the car found in the collection of the Museo Storico Alfa-Romeo is the original, pre-1915 version.

It is also interesting to note that, at the time when it was built, the car was not yet known as an Alfa-Romeo. In 1910, a group of

1 Casucci 1978, pp. 207-208.

businessmen took over the Milan factories built by the French firm Darracq, and founded the Anonima Lombarda Fabbrica Automobili, or ALFA. A year later, they marketed the first Alfa-designed automobile and then, in 1915, relinquished control of the plant to engineer Nicola Romeo. It was after a second restructuring in 1920 that the company and the automobiles it produced began to carry the Alfa-Romeo name.[2]

2   Alfa-Romeo/Vassal 1991, pp. 36-37.

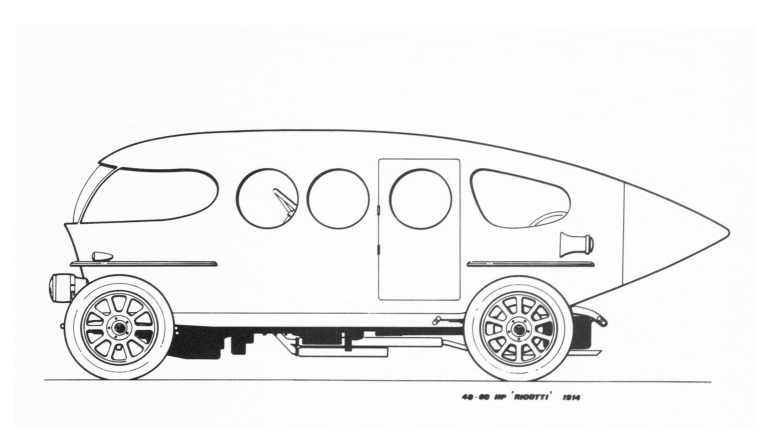

The Alfa 40/60 Ricotti in 1914.

4.

Miller Golden Submarine 1916

ON MAY 8, 1917, *TIME* MAGAZINE PRESENTED THE GOLDEN SUBMARINE, AN amazing racing car constructed entirely by Harry Miller. Since September of the previous year, the American press had been whetting the appetite of motor-racing fans with rumours of this astonishing vehicle.

The unusual automobile had an extremely streamlined shape for the period. Its rounded body was constructed of a sheet of aluminum mounted on a tubular steel chassis. Driver Barney Oldfield, for whom the car had been made, entered the vehicle through a single tiny door on the right side. Once inside, he had to make do with a window area scarcely larger than that found on a First World War armoured car.

The body was painted with gold Duco metallic lacquer, hence its name. The wheels and chassis were not streamlined, and in many ways the car resembled the aerodynamic vehicles of Paul Jaray.

Of course it was no surprise when the Golden Submarine's rounded form led some to joke about the "golden egg," the "percolator" or the "U-boat".[1]

Miller Golden Submarine 1916

ENGINE
Type: straight 4-cylinder, 4 valves per cylinder
Displacement: 4,740 cc. Bore and stroke: 92 mm x 178 mm
Horsepower: 135 hp at 2,950 rpm
DIMENSIONS
Length: 4,580 mm; width: 1,620 mm; height: not provided;
wheelbase: 3,100 mm; weight: 1,140 kg
TRANSMISSION
3-speed manual
PERFORMANCE
Maximum speed: 130 km/h
COLLECTION
Boudeman Collection, Richland, Michigan

The chassis design was unconventional. Lower than usual, it also had a new type of duplex steering system[2] that was both more durable and, above all, more effective. With this vehicle Miller also inaugurated the use of wooden beams to increase chassis rigidity. The car was powered by a large, 4.7-litre, 4-cylinder aluminum engine also developed by Miller. Finally, the suspension featured cantilever springs like those used on the Rolls-Royce Silver Ghost.

The Golden Submarine entered its first race in June 1917 but was forced to withdraw because of a mechanical breakdown. A few weeks later the car proved more effective racing on a hard-packed dirt track, where it won the first of many victories.

Oldfield drove the Golden Submarine through the entire year. The racing car last appeared in the form found here in Springfield, Illinois at the end of 1917. During the race, Oldfield swerved into a railing, piercing the gas tank and causing a fire. Athough he barely

1   Miller/Dees 1981, p. 60.

2   "Duplex steering gear with drag links down each
    side of the frame" ibid., p. 59.

managed to get free of the car, he sustained no injuries. The fire was put out but the cockpit was severely damaged. Oldfield decided to remove what was left of the body and leave the chassis open from behind the firewall.

Oldfield went on to win several more races in the lighter version of the Golden Submarine. In 1918, the car was given a new, more traditional body with an open cockpit.

The car was raced several more times until 1920. It was then shipped to Cuba where it ended its career as a racer. What became of it remains a mystery. At the end of the 1970s, American collector R. J. Boudeman had a replica of the Golden Submarine built from archival photographs and articles.

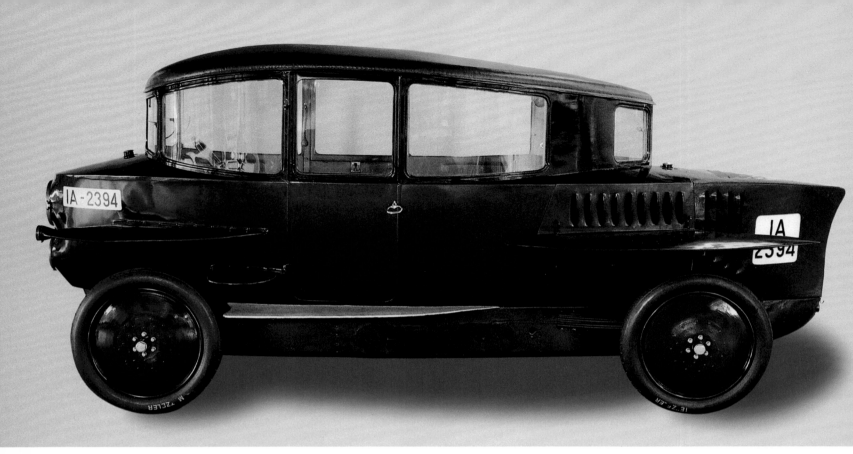

5.

Rumpler Tropfenwagen OA 104 1921

Rumpler *Tropfenwagen* OA 104 1921

ENGINE
Type: 6-cylinder, in a W. Displacement: 2,580 cc. Bore and stroke: 74 mm x 100 mm. Power: 36 hp at 2,000 rpm[2]

DIMENSIONS
Length: 4,550 mm; width: 1,620 mm; height: 1,950 mm; wheelbase: 2,900 mm; weight: 1,375 kg[3]

TRANSMISSION
3-speed manual

PERFORMANCE
Maximum speed: 105 km/h

COLLECTION
Deutsches Museum, Munich

TODAY, THE RUMPLER WOULD BE DESCRIBED AS HAVING AN AERODYNAMIC design, but in the early 1920s the car stood outside any existing frame of reference. These were the automobile's teenage years, a period of growing mechanical reliability and continued public enthusiasm for the touring car, since high-priced sedans were affordable only to the elite.

From 1897 to 1907, the German Edmund Rumpler worked for automobile manufacturers Nesselsdorfer, Daimler and Adler. At Adler, he established a reputation for innovation, developing an oscillating rear-axle assembly that he would patent, and a transmission that was integrated into the engine (transaxle) that would be used in the Adler 40/50, which was shown at the 1905 Frankfurt show.

In 1907, Rumpler established an aircraft manufacturing company (Rumpler Verke-Gesellschaft mbH). One of his creations was the Taube monoplane, much feared by Allied servicemen. After the war he was forbidden to work in the aviation industry, so he returned to the automobile. He had, in fact, been designing a revolutionary automobile since 1915.

In 1921, Rumpler unveiled an automobile that was, to say the least, streamlined. His "teardrop-shaped car" (*Tropfenwagen* in German) created a sensation at the Berlin show. Rumpler's fondness for Symbolism led him to adorn the vehicle with the image of a winged Icarus. Built in Rumpler's Berlin workshops, the car exhibited numerous principles its builder had acquired during his years in aviation design. In fact, Rumpler's stated purpose was to "achieve the least possible air resistance, raise the least possible dust, provide the best fuel consumption and attain the best possible engine efficiency."[1]

Viewed from above, the vehicle resembled a fish. The front end was rounded, and the body's elongated form culminated in a vertical point. To reduce wind resistance, the tires were mounted on solid, rather than spoked, wheels. The headlights were not "stuck on" the fenders, as was the common practice. Instead, Rumpler had integrated two lights into the front of the vehicle. Curved fenders, also a source of resistance, were replaced by horizontal mudguards designed to cut through the air rather than hold it back. The very

1   Rumpler/Büschi 1983, p. 91.

2   Rumpler/Tavard 1977, p. 26.

3   Ibid, p. 31.

long upper fin included a side light. The windshield and the windows in the front section took on the curved lines of the body.

Two side doors provided access to the interior. The driver sat in a central seat located far forward, while three passengers could be accommodated on a bench behind.

The engine was mounted in the rear, in front of the axle. It had three banks of two cylinders mounted in a W; the two side banks were set at about 50° to the central, vertical bank. The water-cooled engine had overhead valves and aluminum pistons. Two oscillating half-axles, mounted on slanting cantilever springs, transmitted the car's 36 hp to the rear wheels. Naturally, Rumpler used the transaxle principle he had developed for Adler in 1905.

A handful of *Tropfenwagens* were manufactured from 1921 to 1924, but the car's futuristic look defied conventional taste. In 1925, Rumpler launched a second generation with the 10/50 PS. Although it had conventional, rounded fenders, it was no more successful.

True, the Rumpler was expensive, costing twice as much as the DKW torpedo, a popular model of the time. As well, its increased speed and greater fuel efficiency were not enough to justify the vehicle's eccentric appearance, especially to a public unaware of the principles of aerodynamics.

In 1926, Rumpler presented a new model, the Front. A conventional looking touring car, it nonetheless sported front-wheel drive and a four-wheel independent suspension. The economic uncertainty of pre-Hitler Germany made commercial success impossible. Edmund Rumpler's automotive adventure was at an end.

Rumpler's efforts cannot be considered a failure, however. In the early 1980s, the Deutsches Museum's Rumpler was subjected to wind-tunnel tests at Volkswagen, and the results were astounding. This 1921 car had a drag coefficient (Cd) of 0.28. This is the same as the 1995 Lexus LS400, which has one of the lowest Cd ratings of any contemporary mass-produced automobile.

The *Tropfenwagen* in Volkswagen's wind-tunnel in the early 1980s.
Photo: Museum für Verkehr und Technik Berlin

6.

Voisin C6 Laboratoire 1923

IN 1922, CONTRARY TO ALL EXPECTATIONS, VOISIN AUTOMOBILES TOOK FIRST, second, third and fifth place in the Touring Grand Prix held by the Automobile Club de France (ACF) in Strasbourg. This was enough to convince Gabriel Voisin to go for the supreme challenge, the French Grand Prix.

The Voisin C6 was a unique automobile characterized by its simplicity. It was built in only six months, thanks to the help of two young engineers: André Lefèvre (who would later design the Citroën *Traction Avant* model) and Marius Bernard, both part of Gabriel's *Grande équipe Voisin*.

The C6, called the *Laboratoire* after the research department, was undeniably aerodynamic in shape, and drew much of its inspiration from the wing of an aircraft. Viewed from the side, the car was equally pointed in both front and rear. From above the look was unusual: the aluminum "fuselage" was mounted on a monocoque chassis built of ash and covered the rear wheels entirely. This dispensed with the need for a differential and gave the car a stunning appearance. The track of the front wheels measured 1.45 metres, but narrowed to only 0.75 metres in the rear.

Voisin C6 *Laboratoire* 1923

ENGINE

Type: in-line, valveless 6 (Knight type), 2 horizontal Zenith carburetors. Displacement: 1,992 cc. Bore and stroke: 62 mm x 110 mm. Horsepower: 75 hp at 5,500 rpm[1]

DIMENSIONS

Length: 4,530 mm; width: 1,500 mm (front) and 750 mmm (back); height: 900 mm; wheelbase: 2,720 mm; weight: 750 kg

TRANSMISSION

3-speed manual

PERFORMANCE

Maximum speed: 180 km/h

COLLECTION

Philipp Moch Collection

The car was also extremely low: its highest point, behind the driver's head, was only 1.6 metres from the ground. The underside was completely flat. Even the four wheels had caps to reduce wind resistance.

The 2.0-litre, 6-cylinder engine was a development of the 4-cylinder built for the Voisin C4, to which two cylinders had simply been added. As in the previous model, it was a Knight valveless engine. The block was made of aluminum, and the compression ratio was increased for racing purposes. The cooling system was also altered by the addition of a water pump. This was powered by a small propeller mounted on an extremely angular grille, a detail that drew much attention at the racetrack.

With a 6-cylinder engine that produced barely 80 hp, the *Laboratoire* seemed very frail compared to the Fiat 850 with its 8-cylinder, 130-hp, supercharged engine. Nonetheless, this 750-kg, "four-wheeled wing" could reach 170 km/h.

---

1   Voisin/Bellu 1978, p. 85.

Adjustments during a trial.

Four Voisin *Laboratoire* cars took to the track for the ACF's French Grand Prix, staged at Tours in June 1923. By the end, the car piloted by Lefèvre managed to come in fifth. As it turned out, the winner was not the Fiat. The honours went to Henry Segrave, who was driving a 110-hp Sunbeam, a car built by two Italians who had taken the Fiat as their inspiration.

Voisin took part in the next year's race with three cars developed from the unusual *Laboratoire*, but the attempt was severely compromised by a series of breakdowns. Voisin would later recognize that even the 1923 fifth place – a triumph in the eyes of the *grande équipe* – had had virtually no effect on sales. For the public, there was simply too great a distance between the *Laboratoire* and Voisin's production models. As historian Serge Bellu points out, Gabriel Voisin called their involvement in racing "unqualified stupidity."[2]

2   Voisin/Bellu 1978, p. 52.

André Lefèvre at the wheel of one of the Voisin C6 *Laboratoires* that took part in the French Grand Prix in June 1923. To his left, Fortin, his mechanic.

7.
Panhard-Levassor 35 CV 1926

At the turn of the century, the Panhard company had abandoned motor racing and turned its efforts to the development of touring cars. In the early 1920s, however, potential commercial advantages would lure Panhard back to the world of motor sports.

By then, however, the marque had neither the financial means nor the technical expertise required to set up a racing team. Instead it decided to concentrate on speed records, an approach well-suited to the reputation of the Panhard 20 CV Sports, among the best French sports cars of its time.

A first competition automobile was unveiled in 1925. It was powered by a modified version of the 4-cylinder, 4.8-litre engine used in Panhard's production car. In June of that year, Marius Breton, engineer for the Marius company, took up a challenge on the Montlhéry speedway. Despite a flat tire, he circled the track at 190.324 km/h, setting three records in the process. Panhard's reaction was enthusiastic.

On August 31, an amateur racing car driver named Ortmans also broke records on the same track. The resulting publicity was much appreciated by Panhard, as was confirmation of the effectiveness of the sleeve-valve engine that the company had adopted in 1911.

The design of Panhard's competition model was nonetheless rather rudimentary. Early models had bodies of copper-studded mahogany planks that ran from the hood to the rear of the car, where they converged. The radiator and hood of the 20 CV Sport were retained. A new aluminum body was designed for a fresh assault on the records in March 1926. Once again, Panhard's efforts were met with great success.

Competition was fierce, however, and the new records did not stand for long. A new competition vehicle was, therefore, unveiled in September 1926. Aptly named "the razor blade," it had an extremely low-set and narrow streamlined body only 55 cm wide. The driver, Breton, set a new record on September 29; however, he was killed during a second set of speed tests held a few days later.

Panhard continued testing and developing "the razor blade," but in 1930 took a new direction. A new automobile was built using the

Panhard-Levassor 35 CV known as *Des Records*, 1926

ENGINE
Type: 8-cylinder in-line, sleeve-valve (Knight type). Displacement: 7,938 cc.[2] Bore and stroke: 95 mm x 140 mm. Horsepower: 235 hp at 3,200 rpm

DIMENSIONS
Length: 5,200 mm; width: 1,730 mm; height: not provided; wheelbase: 3,820 mm; weight: 1,640 kg

TRANSMISSION
4-speed manual

PERFORMANCE
Maximum speed: 214 km/h

COLLECTION
Musée national de l'Automobile de Mulhouse, France, Schlumpf collection

chassis of the 8-cylinder 35 CV Sport. Its body closely resembled that of the 1926 model. As initial test at Arpajon produced encouraging results. The French driver Doré attained a speed of 222 km/h.

Panhard then hired British record-breaker George Eyston, who proceeded to establish four new records, including the hour record, set at 210.393 km/h. Even Panhard's rival manufacturer, Voisin, publicly applauded the achievement, as both Voisin and Panhard were strong proponents of the sleeve-valve engine, denigrated by other manufacturers.

Despite the Depression's negative impact on business, Panhard developed a new car for Eyston. (This car is currently in the Mulhouse collection.) For the first time the front end, which was borrowed from the 8 DS model, was streamlined, and the rear of the body was lowered considerably. Panhard claimed that the new 8-litre engine had an output of 290 hp (although French historian Jacques Rousseau sets the figure at 235 hp).

Eyston would drive the Montlhéry speedway three times, despite blowing a tire during one of the test runs. At the end of 1933 he shattered three records, including the standard for 100 km in 27 minutes and 40.30 seconds.[1] On February 4, 1934, he covered 214.064 km in 60 minutes. Finally, on May 18, he set six all-round world records, and an additional six records for the 5- to 8-litre class. A magnificent way indeed to mark the end of Panhard's venture into the world of competitive motor sports!

1   Panhard/Pérot 1979, p. 104.

8.

Miller 91 1928

In the 1920s, the Indianapolis 500 was the most prestigious motor racing event in the United States.

During this decade, victory at the Indy belonged to two American carmakers, Duesenberg and Miller. Harry Miller's reputation in North America rivalled Ettore Bugatti's in Europe, and the success of the Miller 91 on American soil equalled the achievements of the Bugatti Type 35 on the other side of the Atlantic. Miller's car was so popular that, in 1929, 27 of the 33 contestants on the Indy 500 starting line were driving Miller 91s![1]

Harry Miller had been producing high-performance engines since 1916. Some well-known drivers owed their fame to Miller engines. These included Barney Oldfield with his 1916 Golden Submarine and 1922 Indy winner Jimmy Murphy. The following year, Miller began to build single-and two-seater racing cars under his own name. The result would be a series of victories on American circuits.

In 1926, Indianapolis Speedway officials set the regulation engine displacement to 1.5 litres (about 91 cubic inches). This change coincided with the launching of Miller's masterpiece, the 91. Despite its narrow and elegant body, the Miller 91 was in fact made to a very simple design, one that stressed efficiency first and foremost. Like the other single-seaters that circled the Indy track, the 91 had open wheels and suspension. Some cars did not even have windshields. At that time protective goggles were clearly essential for the driver.

The 91's dual overhead cam, multi-valve engine had a displacement of 91 cubic inches (hence the car's name) and came was equipped with a supercharger. American driver Frank Lockhart won the 1926 Indy 500 driving a 91 with a modified engine that provided 285 hp rather than the standard 154.

Miller offered models of the 91 with either rear-wheel or front-wheel drive, although the latter cost an additional $5,000 US.[2] While the front-wheel drive versions were faster in the straightaways, it was the rear-wheel drive models that came away with the Indy victories (Lockhart in 1926, Louis Meyer in 1928, and Ray Keech in 1929).

Miller 91 1928

ENGINE
Type: in-line 8 cylinder, DOHC, 16 valves, supercharger.
Displacement: 1,491 cc. Bore and stroke: not provided
Horsepower: 154 hp at 7,000 rpm
DIMENSIONS
Length: 3,730 mm; width: 1,630 mm; height: not provided;
wheelbase: not provided; weight: not provided
TRANSMISSION
3-speed manual
PERFORMANCE
Maximum speed: 160 km/h
COLLECTION
Indianapolis Motor Speedway Hall of Fame Museum, Indianapolis

1 Taylor 1991, p. 61.

2 Georgano 1971, p. 539.

No more than about fifty Miller 91s were built from 1926 to 1929, and of those no more than a dozen were front-wheel drive models.[3] In 1929, Miller sold his race car and engine-building firm. He went to work for Erret Loban Cord, where he would develop the front-wheel drive Cord L-29.

3   Ibid.

9.

Auburn 8-120 Boattail 1929

O VER THE YEARS, AUTOMOBILE MANUFACTURERS HAVE BORROWED NUMEROUS design elements from boats as well as airplanes. The best illustration of this is the Boattail style (called "skiff" by French coachbuilders such as Labourdette). The main feature of this style was the pronounced tapering of the body's rear section, which ended in the shape of a bow.

Originally intended to enhance the air flow of race cars, the boattail design was quickly adopted for prestige automobiles by American manufacturers such as Kissel, DuPont, Packard and Duesenberg. It was Auburn, however, that produced the finest boattail designs during the 1920s and 1930s.

Founded in Auburn, Indiana in 1900, the Auburn company remained rather obscure until its takeover by Erret Loban Cord. In 1924, the production of Auburns barely reached six per day, and dozens remained unsold. Cord believed that beautiful automobiles were easier to sell, so he decided to alter the Auburn's appearance and use bright, fashionable colours; it was not long before he had cleared out the remaining inventory. In 1925, Cord introduced a line of Auburns with more powerful, 8-cylinder Lycoming engines. The new cars retained the previous model's vibrant colours, which were accentuated by a two-tone scheme highlighting the belt line. This design would be used by Cord automobiles until 1930.

In 1925, Auburn sales figures showed a twofold increase over 1924 (from 2,000 to 4,000 units, approximately). In 1926, figures doubled again. By 1929, they reached 18,000 units, a record year for Auburn.[1]

Since Cord relied heavily on appearance to sell automobiles, he kept a close watch on his competitors. At this time the American manufacturer Stutz was offering a Boattail model, the Black Hawk, which had acquired a solid reputation as a performance automobile. Cord saw the this car as a trendsetter. Since the engines of his Auburns were no match for Stutz's, Cord concentrated on aesthetics to draw public attention.

In 1928, Erret Cord unveiled his first two Auburn Speedster two-seaters, the 8-88 and 8-115 models, They came with 8-cylinder

Auburn 8-120 Boattail 1929

ENGINE
Type: in-line 8-cylinder, Schebler carburetor
Displacement: 4,894 cc. Bore and stroke: 82.5 mm x 114 mm.
Horsepower: 125 hp at 3,600 rpm[2]

DIMENSIONS
Length: 4,572 mm; width: 1,803 mm; height: 1,422 mm; wheelbase: 3,277 mm; weight: 1,680 kg

TRANSMISSION
3-speed manual

PERFORMANCE
Maximum speed: 145 km/h

COLLECTION
Richard Grenon, Au-Temps-Tic Auto, Sainte-Anne-de-Bellevue, Quebec

1   Brown (ed.) 1993, p. 207.
2   Naul 1978, pp. 22-23.

engines and were listed at $1,695 and $2,195 US respectively,[3] less than half the cost of a Stutz Black Hawk. In 1929, he added the 8-120 model, built on a 3.3-metre wheelbase. This top-of-the-line Speedster was listed starting at $1,895 US.[4]

The bodies of Cord's Speedsters were created by Russian stylist Alexis de Sakhnoffsky, who had moved to the United States in 1927.[5] He went on to work for the Cord group on a permanent basis.

Some fifty 8-120 Speedsters are said to have been built in 1929. Three less expensive models, the 8-88, 8-90 and 8-115, were also listed in the catalogue that year. No more than 20 8-120s are still in existence today. One of these, acquired by a Quebec resident during the Depression, was severely damaged during a fire in 1938. In the early 1990s, it was completely restored by Quebecker Richard Grenon. Once again, we can see the original bright colours and the two-tone paint job, and be dazzled by the orange leather seats!

Like many other boattails, the 8-120 featured a side trunk designed to hold golf bags.

3 Auburn/Kimes 1978, p. 72.

4 Ibid.

5 Tubbs 1978, p. 80.

10.
Alfa-Romeo 6C 1750 Gran Sport 1930

THE ALFA-ROMEO 6C 1750 WAS ONE OF THE MOST FAMOUS AUTOMOBILES ever produced under the sign of the four-leaf clover. It was developed mainly by engineer Vittorio Jano, who had been lured away from Fiat by Enzo Ferrari, then working for Alfa. From 1923 to 1937, Jano developed a line of extraordinary touring cars, of which the 1750 was the crowning achievement.

When he began working for Alfa-Romeo in the early 1920s, Jano was assigned the task of injecting new life into its rather lacklustre line of products. At the Milan Motor Show of 1925, he launched the 6C 1500, a light touring automobile with a 1.5-litre engine that, depending on the version, produced between 44 hp and 76 hp. In 1928, the Campari/Ramponi team scored Alfa's first victory in the *Mille Miglia* driving a 6C 1500 with an 84-hp engine.

In 1929, the 1500 was replaced by the 1750. The basic concept of a short chassis coupled with a powerful engine was retained and improved upon. Unveiled that same year at the Rome Motor Show, the 1750 came in a number of different versions, including the Turismo, the Sport and the Super Sport. The latter two became the Gran Turismo and the Gran Sport in 1930.

Alfa-Romeo 6C 1750 Gran Sport 1930

ENGINE
Type: in-line 6-cylinder, DOHC, one Memini dual venturi carburetor. Displacement: 1,752 cc. Bore and stroke: 65 mm x 88 mm. Horsepower: 64 hp at 4,500 rpm (85 hp with Roots supercharger)

DIMENSIONS
Length: 4,050 mm; width: 1,730 mm; height: 1,420 mm; wheelbase: 2,745 mm; weight: 840 kg

TRANSMISSION
4-speed manual

PERFORMANCE
Maximum speed: 145 km/h

COLLECTION
Museo Storico Alfa-Romeo, Arese, Italy

The Turismo, the mildest of the three, featured a 3,100-mm wheelbase and a 46-hp engine, while the Sport/Gran Turismo had a shorter, 2,920-mm wheelbase and a 55-hp engine. The more exciting Super Sport/Gran Sport had a very short, 2,740 mm chassis and a 64-hp, twin-cam engine. When equipped with a Roots supercharger, the motor's output reached 85 hp. The Gran Sport chassis was produced with bodywork by design greats Castagna, Pinin Farina, Touring and Zagato, among others. It was Zagato who built the body for the 1750.

The rather narrow passenger compartment was suited to no more than average-sized riders, although the tiny doors had hollows to provide the outside arm some freedom of movement. As the doors were also without windows, this was not a car for rainy day outings.

The 1750's architecture was of a classic design. The chassis consisted of two pressed side rails and crossmembers. The car had

two beam axles and a semi-elliptical spring suspension with friction damper.

The lower part of the 6-cylinder straight engine was made of a light alloy, but the cylinder head and engine block were of cast iron to simplify the manufacturing process. The engine in the Super Sport/Gran Sport models featured twin overhead camshafts, with the valves angled at 90°. The cams were driven by a vertical shaft connected to the crankshaft.

When fitted with the Roots supercharger, this under-1,000 kg roadster could reach a speed of 145 km/h. On the road, however, the automobile displayed a tendency to oversteer that precluded mass appeal.

The 1750 dominated the racing circuits from 1929 to 1932. Thanks to the talent of driving greats such as Nuvolari, Varzi, Ramponi and Campari, Alfa-Romeo was unbeatable at the *Mille Miglia*, save in 1931.

From 1929 to 1933, Alfa-Romeo built 2,000 1750s, including 369 Super Sport/Gran Sport chassis[1]. Between 1966 and 1968, at the suggestion of Italian magazine *Quattroruote*, Alfa-Romeo produced 92 replica Gran Sports. These "4R Zagatos" used the mechanics and chassis of the Guilia Spider 1600, but retained the splendid appearance of the Gran Sport.

1   Alfa-Romeo/Gary 1991, p. 54.

At the 1930 *Mille Miglia*, the duo of Nuvolari and Guidotti in the Alfa-Romeo 1750 *Gran Sport*.

11.

Mercedes-Benz SSK Trossi 1932

At the end of the 1920s, Germany witnessed the introduction of several new sports cars. The Mercedes-Benz SS, SSK and SSKL models would quickly become famous.

The SSK (for *Super Sports Kurz*, [short]) was introduced in 1928. It was recognizable by the exceptionally low chassis, long hood, and the three exhaust pipes that protruded from the hood on the passenger side. A further distinguishing feature was the spare tires mounted on the very short rear section of the body. This was so short that some people sarcastically remarked that it was "the biggest car with the smallest trunk".[1]

The SSK rapidly won sporting acclaim thanks to its victories in Grand Prix racing, the 1930 European hill-climb championship, and many other contests.

Mercedes-Benz SSK Trossi 1932

ENGINE

Type: straight 6 with a Roots supercharger, 2 Pallas carburetors.
Displacement: 7,020 cc. Bore and stroke: 100 mm x 150 mm.
Horsepower: 300 hp at 3,400 rpm

DIMENSIONS

Length: 4,775 mm; width: 1,803 mm; height: 1,422 mm;
wheelbase: 2,946 mm; weight: 1,397 kg

TRANSMISSION

4-speed manual

PERFORMANCE

Maximum speed: 200 km/h

COLLECTION

Ralph Lauren Collection

The history of the SSK did not take place on the racecourse, however. It began at the end of 1929, when a bare chassis numbered 36038 was shipped to Tokyo. After about a year, the car returned to Europe, going to Milan Mercedes dealer Carlo Saporiti. He had the automobile for almost two years before it was purchased.

The buyer was Count Carlo Felice Trossi, an Italian nobleman from Piedmont and an automobile enthusiast.[2] From 1932 to 1948, "Didi," as the Count was known to his friends, had a brilliant motor racing career, winning numerous competitions at the wheel of Alfa-Romeo, Maserati and Mercedes-Benz cars. Driving an SSK, he came second in the 1932 Turbian Grand Prix in France's Alpes-Maritimes. Trossi was also chairman of the *Scuderia* Ferrari from 1932 to 1936,[3] but the title was purely honorary; Ferrari directed operations while Trossi raised money.

History does not tell us why Trossi decided to have the coachwork for his SSK chassis done in England. Stock SSKs were designed to be functional, which gave them a severe appearance that was, doubtless, too severe for Trossi who wanted a more elegant car. He presented his plans to an obscure British coachbuilder, Willie White.

The result was spectacular. Unlike the factory-made SSKs, the Trossi had fluid forms as sophisticated as those found on the most

1 Mercedes-Benz/Scott-Moncrieff 1979, p. 375.

2 Ferrari/Yates 1991, pp. 65-66.

3 Cutter and Fendall 1973, p. 614.

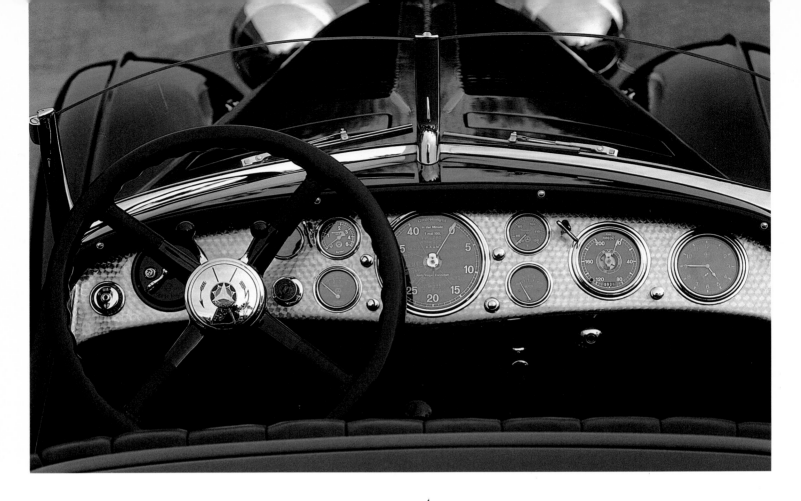

beautiful touring cars built by Italian coachbuilders such as Zagato and Touring. The body was deep black, as were the wire wheels and the leather upholstery of the interior seats. Along with the chrome radiators, the shine of the large, polished copper brake drums added a contrasting element to the overall black.

White had done a remarkable job. The hood was formed to meet the V-shaped radiator. The hood and the fenders had been lowered to convey an impression of greater speed. Whereas the stock SSK had motorcycle-type fenders, White had designed long wings for the Trossi that continued all the way to the rear, completely hiding the chassis visible on the stock model. Even the small ridges on top of the rear fenders melded perfectly with the rear bodywork. White went so far as to place the Mercedes three-branched star at the very bottom of the rear fenders.

This SSK was equipped with a 7-litre engine of the type generally reserved for Mercedes' racing models. A straight 6 with a Roots supercharger, the engine generated 300 hp, which was sufficient to propel the SSK at 200 km/h.

Felice Trossi sold and then repurchased the SSK twice before his death in 1949. The car went through the hands of various owners before being purchased by the Ralph Lauren Collection in 1988. There it was completely restored by Massachusetts specialist Paul Russell.

12.

Bugatti 46 Coach Profilé 1933

THE 46 BUGATTI WAS INTRODUCED BY THE MULHOUSE MANUFACTURER IN 1929 as a means of entering the luxury car market. It was to compete with automobiles like the Hispano-Suiza and the Rolls-Royce. In retrospect, of course, the company seems to have chose a rather inopportune moment to launch its new product. In any case, the Type 46 was, with the exception of the Royale itself, the largest car ever built by Bugatti. It was to become the personal favorite of *Le Patron*.

Following the Royale in the hierarchy of Bugatti automobiles, the Type 46 was nicknamed the "Little Royale". The *Autocar's Buyers' Guide of 1934 Cars* helps put this in perspective. The guide tells us that the Royale's chassis was priced at £5,250, while the Type 46 cost £975, plus £200 for the supercharged version. Looked at from another angle, the Royale offered the prospective car buyer 6.4 litres of additional engine displacement over the Type 46, a wheelbase 32 inches longer, and a track 8 inches wider. The Guide also mentions that an Austin Seven two-seater was listed at £105 and that the chassis of a Rolls-Royce 40-50 was priced at £1,800, double the price of a Type 46 chassis, but only one-third the price of a Royale chassis.[1]

Bugatti 46 Coach *Profilé* 1933

ENGINE
Type: in-line 8-cylinder, OHC, 3 valves per cylinder,
1 Smith-Barriquand carburetor. Displacement: 5,359 cc.
Bore and stroke: 81 mm x 130 mm. Horsepower: 140 hp

DIMENSIONS
Length: 4,780 mm; width: 1,920 mm; height: unavailable;
wheelbase: 3,500 mm; weight: 1,150 kg

TRANSMISSION
3-speed manual

PERFORMANCE
Maximum speed: 160 km/h

COLLECTION
Musée national de l'Automobile de Mulhouse, France, Schlumpf Collection

Luxury car enthusiasts were struck by the 46's quiet and smooth-running 8-cylinder engine, which gave the car a top speed close to 150 km/h. The car's road-holding abilities and comfort were also far superior to those of the average automobile. To the delight of Bugatti enthusiasts, the supercharged Type 46 became available in 1930.

Unlike the engines in the Type 38 and Type 44 models, which were in fact composed of two 4-cylinder blocks set end to end, the block of the Type 46's engine was cast in a single piece.

The "Little Royale" shared some of the "Big" Royale's technical features. The crankshaft was set low in the engine block, in a removable aluminum casing. The 3-speed gearbox was integrated with the rear axle. The technical complexity of the latter arrangement was noted by many, who felt it was not designed to be handled by amateur mechanics.

1   Bugatti/Barker 1971, p. 117.

No one knows why Ettore Bugatti consistently refused to equip the 46 with hydraulic brakes. It is easy to imagine, however, how difficult it must have been for a driver to bring this car to a quick stop in an emergency.

Many Type 46 automobiles featured prestige coachwork by such renowned designers as Binder and Kellner. The long chassis of the 46 allowed some coachbuilders to fully indulge their design fantasies. Coachwork for many other Type 46 cars was handled by Bugatti's Mulhouse works.

Ettore Bugatti's son, Jean, used a Type 46 chassis to build a "super-streamlined" model with fluid lines. The 2+2 displayed a truncated, curved silhouette, with rear fenders that extended beyond the back of the car. This design was in some ways similar to the amazing Bugatti Atlantic that Jean Bugatti would create a few years later.

The Type 46 left the factory with wire wheels or, occasionally, chrome disk wheels. Alloy rims based on the Royale's were also provided for the "Little Royale".

By the time Bugatti halted production of the car in 1936, the Molsheim factory had built fewer than 500 Type 46 Bugattis.

13.

Alfa-Romeo B Aerodinamica 1934

THE HISTORY OF THE *AERODINAMICA* IS LINKED TO THE STORY OF ENZO Ferrari who, beginning in 1920, worked with Alfa-Romeo for some twenty years.[1] In 1923, he succeeded in enticing designer Vittorio Jano away from Fiat. Jano had been director of Fiat's racing division when that company's cars were Grand Prix winners.[2] At Alfa, Jano developed the 2.0-litre P2 2-seat racer to replace the P1, designed shortly before. Unlike the P1, which had never attained its full potential, the P2 rapidly became a major contender on the racing scene.

Alfa-Romeo B *Aerodinamica* 1934

ENGINE
Type: straight 8. Displacement: 2,905 cc. Bore and stroke: 68 mm x 100 mm. Horsepower: 255 hp at 5,400 rpm

DIMENSIONS
Length: 4,370 mm; width: 1,600 mm; height: 1,400 mm; wheelbase: 2,650 mm; weight: 720 kg

TRANSMISSION
4-speed manual

PERFORMANCE
Maximum speed: 290 km/h

COLLECTION
Museo Storico Alfa-Romeo, Arese, Italy

In the early 1930s, Italian dictator Benito Mussolini hoped to impress the rest of Europe by providing Italy with the most powerful Grand Prix cars. He therefore financed Alfa-Romeo's production of these unbeatable automobiles. (Hitler, who had the same idea, provided substantial financial support to Mercedes-Benz and Auto-Union for racing-car development.)

In 1932, Vittorio Jano unveiled the Tipo B, also known as the P3.[3] The car was a one-seater equipped with a 2.6-litre engine with dual superchargers (displacement would later be increased to 3.0 litres). The first versions, equipped with 215-hp engines, could reach speeds of 225 km/h. With talented drivers like Tazio Nuvolari, Rudolf Caracciola, Luigi Fagioli and Louis Chiron at the wheel, the P3 soon surpassed its rivals.

In 1933, Alfa-Romeo announced that it was withdrawing from competition. The company was in such deep financial trouble that it was nationalized shortly afterwards.[4] This made the situation difficult for Ferrari, who had led the official stable since 1929. It was all very well that the Ferrari stable had the best drivers, but their cars were starting to age and were being beaten more and more frequently. The new, powerful German competitors, Mercedes-Benz and Auto-Union, would soon arrive and take over the scene.

Ferrari therefore had to develop a new car capable of beating his German rivals. Derived from the 1932 Alfa-Romeo P3, the *Aerodinamica* had a highly streamlined body with bold design by aeronautics engineer[5] and stylist Pallavicino de Breda.[6] The

1 Ferrari/Yates 1991, pp. 21-25.

2 Alfa-Romeo/Hull 1971, p. 51.

3 Alfa-Romeo/Orsini, p. 123.

4 Ibid., p. 124.

5 Ibid., p. 126.

6 Alfa-Romeo/Hull 1971, p. 110.

streamlining was intended to increase the car's speed. Equipped with a 3.0-litre, 8-cylinder engine that provided an extra 40-hp over other P3 engines, the *Aerodinamica* could beat a conventional P3's speed by 20 km/h.

Only one Tipo B *Aerodinamica* was built; French driver Guy Moll drove it to victory in the Avus Grand Prix in 1934. The car was to have been driven by the stable's top pilot, Italian Achille Varzi; however, he refused because of the strong vibrations that could be felt through the controls during testing. For Moll, however, the situation provided a unique opportunity.

With the arrival of the new German machines, the dominance of Alfa-Romeo's Ferrari stable soon came to an end. Mercedes-Benz began the new Grand Prix season with its W25 model, winning a first victory in the contested Eifelrennan race. Although Chrion, Varzi and the Trossi/Moll team secured the top three positions in the next race, this victory would turn out to be the swan song of the *Scuderia* Tipo Bs. The shape of the B *Aerodinamica* would nonetheless inspire Enzo Ferrari and his team to produce the famous Alfa-Romeo *Bimotore*, an impressive Grand Prix one-seater equipped with two 8-cylinder engines, one in front and one in the rear. It first appeared on the track in the Tripoli Grand Prix in 1936.[7]

(Top)
Count Trossi, the engineer Gobbato, the driver Guidotti, *Commandatore* Ferrari, the engineer Pallavicino, *Commandatore* Yano and several other people gathered around the Alfa-Romeo.

(Above)
Guidotti at the wheel of the 1934 Alfa-Romeo B *Aerodinamica*

---

7   Casucci 1981, p. 49.

14.

Chrysler Airflow CU 1934

COMMERCIALLY SPEAKING, THE CHRYSLER AIRFLOW MUST RANK AMONG THE most unsuccessful cars in history. Technically, however, the Airflow was a major step forward, marking the first time that an American manufacturer had mass-produced a streamlined automobile.

The idea of exploring the use of aerodynamics came from Carl Breer, one of three Chrysler engineers (known as the "three musketeers") responsible for developing new products under the leadership of Walter Percy Chrysler. In 1927, Breer began a project to study the effects of air on various shapes. With the help of Orville Wright, he constructed the first wind tunnel at Chrysler's research centre in Highland Park, Michigan. Before long, an important discovery was made... by accident. After a long day of tests, a wind-tunnel technician had the idea of placing a car backwards in the tunnel. The standard tests were run and, to everyone's astonishment, the car turned out to be more aerodynamically efficient backwards than forwards. The wind-tunnel tests continued until 1931.

For a time, the test results suggested that the company should consider a rear-mounted engine; this was rejected as being too far ahead of its time. In 1932, a first working prototype was constructed. It was named the Trifon Special after the technician who built it.

Two years later, on January 6, 1934, the Chrysler Corporation unveiled the Airflow with much fanfare at the New York Auto Show. The launching was overshadowed, however, by the arrival of Buckminster Fuller driving the futuristic Dymaxion automobile.[1] Parked in front of Grand Central Palace, where the show was being held, the Dymaxion's teardrop shape made the Airflow look almost conventional.

This was far from true, however. The Airflow's rounded hood, flanked by two elongated vertical forms holding the headlights, was like a gleaming aluminum slide. The rear wheels were covered by fender skirts. The engine, either a 6- or 8-cylinder model, was mounted directly above the tubular front axle, rather than behind it. This unusual arrangement made it possible to give the car a large

Chrysler Airflow CU 1934

ENGINE
Type: in-line 8, with side valves, Stromberg carburetor.
Displacement: 4,895 cc. Bore and stroke: 82.6 mm x 114.3 mm.
Horsepower: 122 hp at 3,400 rpm

DIMENSIONS
Length: 5,080 mm; width: 1,930 mm; height: 1,676 mm; wheelbase: 3,124 mm; weight: 1,695 kg

TRANSMISSION
3-speed manual

PERFORMANCE
Maximum speed: 143 km/h

COLLECTION
The William F. Harrah Foundation National Automobile Museum, Reno, Nevada

1 Chrysler/Murray et al. 1973, p. 7.

passenger compartment. The Airflow was undoubtedly the first Chrysler car to adopt the principle of a "cab-forward" passenger compartment, 58 years before the Chrysler LH. In some ways, the Airflow's body resembled that of the first streamlined Tatra from Czechoslovakia.

The Airflow's steel-tube frame with welded-on body panels was another first for the American industry, which had yet to adopt the idea of all-steel bodywork.

For the magazine *Harper's Bazaar*, the Airflow's revolutionary aesthetics "took your breath away",[2] but for most Americans the car was simply grotesque. The public was not ready for such a radical design. The car's reputation was also affected by delays in supply, leading to a host of rumours about mechanical difficulties that were spread by Chrysler's competitors, headed by General Motors.[3]

As well, in 1934, the Jaray Streamline company launched a suit against Chrysler for marketing an automobile with a "streamlined

2 Kimes and Clark 1985, p. 281.

3 Chrysler/Murray et al. 1973, p. 25.

body." The Hungarian Paul Jaray, famous for his application of aerodynamics to automobiles, had in 1927, obtained a patent for a more or less vague concept of an aerodynamic automobile body. The dispute was resolved out of court at great cost in 1935, but could not help but diminish the already tarnished reputation of the Airflow.[4]

The Airflow was sold under the Chrysler and DeSoto brand names until 1937, but starting in 1935 a number of more conventional stylistic elements were added to the car, including a more prominent and vertical grille.

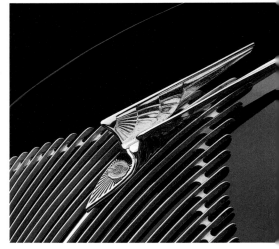

4   Chrysler/Murray et al. 1973, p. 7.

15.

Voisin C25 Aérodyne 1935

THE VOISIN *AÉRODYNE* CREATED A SENSATION AT THE 1934 SALON DE PARIS. Its rounded shape reflected Gabriel Voisin's extensive experience in aircraft design, and was enhanced by a judicious colour scheme. The five-passenger sedan also sported an innovation guaranteed to improve passenger comfort: a sliding roof. A motor in the baggage compartment could slide the roof back, in one piece, all the way to the rear bumper. The roof was also fitted with "portholes" that allowed the maximum light to enter the passenger compartment, no matter what the roof's position. No need for a convertible with a sedan like this!

Voisin C25 *Aérodyne* 1935

ENGINE

Type: in-line 6-cylinder, sleeve valve (Knight type). Displacement: 2,992 cc. Bore and stroke: 76 mm x 110 mm. Horsepower: 100 hp at 3,550 rpm[2]

DIMENSIONS

Length: 4,780 mm; width: 1,600 mm; height: not provided; wheelbase: 3,280 mm; weight: 1,200 kg

TRANSMISSION

2-speed manual

PERFORMANCE

Maximum speed: 140 km/h

COLLECTION

Château de Vincy collection, Switzerland

The slightly rounded but very vertical radiator carried the marque's trademark "Cocotte," and to some extent seemed to contradict the body's otherwise resolutely aerodynamic appearance.

It was doubtless this uncompromising outlook on Voisin's part that brought him closer to the architect Le Corbusier, who was seven years his junior.[1]

In the early 1930s, all automobile manufacturers had suffered heavy losses as a result of the 1929 Crash and subsequent Depression. Voisin was not spared, and sales figures declined year after year. Despite this, Voisin was still driven by a passion for innovation. He spearheaded the development of a V12 engine designed with a prototype in mind. However, the project did not come to fruition. Voisin's "laboratory" next tested a front-wheel-drive prototype powered by a V8 engine, but this idea was also abandoned. An even more eccentric project involved equipping a sedan with a central radial engine and wheels arranged in a diamond shape! It, too, never saw the light of day.

The somewhat more sedate C25 made its appearance at the end of 1934. While its profile was pleasing to some, others found it unsettling. The luggage compartment merged with the rounded body, while the small, narrow doors opened into an elegant passenger compartment. The driver faced a lacquered dashboard laden with buttons and dials that controlled even the shock absorbers. The automobile's 2-speed manual transmission featured the new

1   Voisin/Bellu 1986, p. 84.

2   Rousseau and Caron 1993, entry 394.

Voisin–Cotal electromagnetic preselector. Although this was designed to ease gear-shifting, it still required great dexterity.[3]

The automobile was equipped with a 6-cylinder, Knight valveless
engine identical to the one used in the C24. Voisin was to remain
true to the Knight engine throughout his career. In 1937, Voisin's
financial situation forced him to sell the company to a group of
Belgian investors. The make would survive for another two years.

3   Voisin/Courteault 1991, p. 162.

16.

Lancia Astura Pinin Farina 1936

Lancia introduced the Astura in 1931. It was first offered as a four- or six-passenger sedan. As the successor to the famous Lambda – the world's first mass-produced car with a monocoque chassis and independent front suspension – the Astura was not destined for racing. The first models were classic city vehicles that soon became popular among Mussolini's government officials. The 2.6-litre V8 engine was similar to the ones found in the final Lambda models, but the Astura benefitted from an improved version of the independent front suspension. This first generation of Asturas was sold until 1935.

Over these four years, the Lancia Astura came to be known in Italy as a luxury car. When the second generation of Asturas appeared in 1936, several coachbuilders would take its long wheelbase chassis as a basis for various styling exercises. Among them were Battista Pinin Farina's coachbuilding experts, who produced a number of particularly elegant streamlined bodies on the Astura chassis.

Aerodynamic automobiles were all the rage among the wealthy; as an added incentive the Astura's engine was increased to 3 litres. Some Astura coupes and convertibles were equipped with bodies so streamlined as to be bizarre, to say the least. The model shown here, however, is a sterling example of the design excellence that could be achieved by Italian coachbuilders.

This 1936 "aerodynamic cabriolet" included some traditional elements found on the stock models, including the running boards (albeit quite discreet here) and the "shell" headlights (i.e., not yet built into the fenders). The overall look nonetheless integrated various elongated elements that were suggestive of motion.

The amount of chrome on the body varied depending on the model. Some had massive chrome mudguards in front of the rear fenders. Others were equipped with fender skirts with enormous chrome disks set at the mid-points of the wheels. On some a wide chrome molding covered the running board between the fenders, while on others the ventilation slits on the hood were chromed.

Lancia Astura Pinin Farina 1936

ENGINE
Type: 17.5° V8. Displacement: 2,972 cc. Bore and stroke: 75 mm x 85 mm. Horsepower: 82 hp at 4,400 rpm[1]

DIMENSIONS
Length: 5,500 mm; width: 1,800 mm; height: 1,500 mm; wheelbase: not provided; weight: not provided

TRANSMISSION
4-speed manual

PERFORMANCE
Maximum speed: 130 km/h[2]

COLLECTION
Pininfarina

---

1 Lancia/Frostick 1976, p. 203.

2 Ibid., p. 203.

Most models had impressive, chrome-decorated wheels ornamented with a powerful, concentric circle design. Combined with the brilliance of the plating, this decoration served to lighten the sometimes heavy appearance of large bodies like the one on this convertible, especially those painted in darker colours. The ornamental nature of these chrome elements was reinforced by a length of molding that extended from the radiator all the way to the bottom of the trunk lid in the rear. This "continuous line" not only served to lower the belt line, but its plunge to the car's rear extremity added to the feeling of movement.

The V-shaped windshield enhanced the car's aerodynamic look. To meet the expectations of contemporary drivers, the windshield was in two sections, each of which could be lowered independently to the front to give an "open-air" driving experience like the one provided by the Astura's predecessors. Not surprisingly, coachbuilt Asturas often took top honours for style during the late 1930s.

17.

Panhard-Levassor Dynamic 130 X76 1937

THE PANHARD DYNAMIC WAS UNVEILED IN 1936, ON THE FIFTIETH anniversary of Panhard-Levassor, the dean of French automobile manufacturers.

The Dynamic, a virtual sculpture on wheels, was the work of stylist Louis Bionier.[1] Its futuristic silhouette reflected a new era in automobile design. In fact, the creation of the Dynamic followed the development of two equally daring and innovative automobiles, the Chrysler Airflow and the Peugeot 402. When introduced two years before, they had been the first production sedans to feature aerodynamic styling.

Bionier's design went further, however. The Dynamic's Art Deco look relied on much elaborate and fanciful streamlining, accentuated by the audacious use of two-tone paint on the deluxe models. The front and rear wheels were partly hidden by fender skirts. Small curved windows on either side of the windshield maximized visibility. This avant-garde feature was retained from the Panhard Panoramic, the Dynamic's predecessor.

The running boards were less prominent, foreshadowing their imminent disappearance. As if this design were not sufficiently evocative, Bionier decorated the engine hoods with air intakes whose shape recalled the wings on Mercury's hat.

Not everyone agreed on the Dynamic's aesthetic qualities. As Benoît Pérot reminds us in his history of the marque: "Some found it resembled a corpulent pachyderm, the ultimate in bad taste, while others appreciated its magnificence, originality and aerodynamic silhouette."[2] Audacity has its price.

The designers' specifications were unequivocal: the design was "to provide six travellers with equal and hitherto unprecedented comfort."[3] Hence the great width of the Dynamic, allowing three people to fit comfortably on either of its two bench seats.

The central steering wheel of the Dynamic also created a sensation. This innovation was a logical consequence of the desire to maximize usable space in the passenger compartment.

Panhard-Levassor Dynamic 130 X76 1937

ENGINE
Type: valveless in-line 6-cylinder (Knight type).
Displacement: 2,516 cc. Bore and stroke: 72 mm x 103 mm.
Horsepower: 65 hp at 3,500 rpm[4]

TRANSMISSION
4-speed manual

DIMENSIONS
Length: 5,100 mm; width: 2,050 mm; height: 1,750 mm; wheelbase: 2,800 mm; weight: 1,400 kg

PERFORMANCE
Maximum speed: 115 km/h

COLLECTION
Musée Henri-Malartre, Lyon, France

1 In his book *Panhard, la doyenne d'avant-garde*, Benoît Pérot spells this name with one "n"; Jacques Rousseau in his *Guide de l'automobile française* spells it "Bionner."

2 Panhard/Pérot 1979, p. 164.

3 Ibid., p. 162.

4 Rousseau and Caron 1993, entry 231.

Pininfarina's Ethos III prototype (1993) would also use this concept, but apply it more efficiently.

Imagine, however, the difficulty of driving a 2-metre-wide vehicle from a central position, with your view obstructed by an excessively long hood. The inevitable blind driving this implied made passing other automobiles difficult. As well, to reach the central driving position, the driver was forced to slide across a long bench seat and, once there, found it sorely lacking in lateral support. Consumer resistance resulted in the Dynamic's steering wheel being returned to the left on the 1939 models.

Five body designs appear in the company's catalogue from 1936 to 1939. The Dynamic 140 Major, seen here in the 4-place coach version, was also offered as a long coupe cabriolet version, on a 2,800-mm wheelbase chassis. A short coupe, called the Dynamic 130 Junior (1936-1937), used a 2,600-mm wheelbase chassis, while the sedan and the limousine models both have a longer chassis, with a 3,000-mm wheelbase.

The chassis used monocoque construction and was welded electrically for greater rigidity. This was the first time this process – adopted by Citroën for its "Traction" models in 1934 – was used on a prestige French automobile. The Dynamic also featured a 4-wheel independent suspension and a 4-speed transmission. The hydraulic

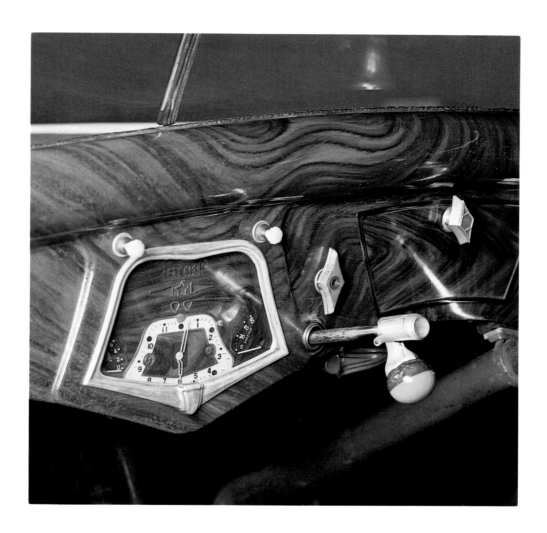

drum brakes were equipped with a self-regulating proportioning valve.

Mechanically, the Panhard remained true to tradition. The 6-cylinder engine was "valveless" (using the American Knight system) with an aluminum cylinder head and twin downdraft carburetors. The Dynamic 140 had a 2.9-litre, 82-hp engine, while the smaller Dynamic 130 (Junior) featured a 2.5-litre, 75-hp engine. The 1938-1939 Dynamic 160, however, was capable of reaching a speed of 140 km/h with its 3.8-litre, 105-hp powerplant.

The Dynamic was to be the last valveless Panhard. At that time, the performance of engines with valves was improving rapidly. The Knight system's domination in terms of power output and quiet running was soon to be a thing of the past.

With the outbreak of war in August 1939, military equipment replaced automobiles on Panhard's production lines. Once the war was over, the company geared its production to the needs of a devastated French nation.

18.

Cord 810 Westchester 1936

FOR ALL INTENTS AND PURPOSES, THE CORD 810 WAS ERRET LOBAN CORD'S swan song. A superb automobile, revolutionary in many respects, it was simply not successful enough to save the American business-man's small empire.

The Cord 810 Westchester, which was unveiled at the New York Motor Show in November 1935[1], was already a bold departure. The design team was led by Gordon Buehrig, who had been responsible for the Auburn Speedster. The body displayed very pronounced curves but, unlike the Chrysler Airflow, the Cord's design was pleasing and balanced.

The futuristic design was restrained in its use of chrome, but the retractable headlights, a North American first, attracted much attention wherever the car was shown. The aerodynamic vehicle could be purchased as a sedan or a convertible. The Cord's attractive body had only one drawback: the small, high windshield.

Under the coffin-shaped hood, the 4.7-litre Lycoming V8 generated 125 horsepower and powered the front wheels. This was unique among American automobiles. After Cord shut down, Americans would have to wait until 1966 before they could purchase a domestic front-wheel-drive automobile, the Oldsmobile Toronado.

In 1937, the car was renamed the 812. The addition of a centri-fugal supercharger increased the engine's horsepower to 170, making the Beverly Sedan version one of the fastest cars in the country. Acceleration from 0 to 100 km/h took 14 seconds, and top speed was 180 km/h.[2] The thoroughbred look of these models was enhanced by the chrome exhaust pipes that emerged from the hood on the passenger side.

The V8 was more compact than the L29 straight 8 engine that powered the first Cord. The 810/812 also sported a new independent front suspension with trailing arms.

The preselector transmission allowed the driver to select the desired gear by first moving a small gear lever found on the steering column, and then pressing down on the clutch. This system was not particularly fast. It did encourage visions of a day when transmis-sions would be both entirely automatic and instantaneous.

Cord 810 Westchester 1936

ENGINE

Type: V8, with side-valves, Stromberg carburetors. Displacement: 4,732 cc. Bore and stroke: 88.9 mm x 95.3 mm. Horsepower: 125 hp

DIMENSIONS:

Length: 5,080 mm; width: 1,829 mm; height: 1,600 mm; wheelbase 3,175 mm; weight: 1,750 kg

TRANSMISSION:

4-speed manual with pre-selector

PERFORMANCE:

Maximum speed: not provided

COLLECTION:

The William F. Harrah Foundation National Automobile Museum, Reno, Nevada

---

1 Ludvigsen and Burgess-Wise 1979, p. 54.

2 Stein 1970, p. 125.

The Cord's main difficulty stemmed from poor assembly and unreliable systems. These were not up to the standards that the high price implied, so potential purchasers were put off. The Westchester was more expensive than a Cadillac Fleetwood Touring Sedan. With the optional supercharger, priced at $2,000, it cost as much as a long-wheelbase Cadillac Fleetwood Town Car limousine. Of course, the Cord had been designed as a "baby Duesenberg," so the price was supposedly no object.

When production stopped on August 7, 1937, the Cord factory had manufactured less than 3,000 Cord 810s and 812s. The end of Cord, after Auburn and Duesenberg, marked the collapse of the automobile empire founded by Erret Loban Cord ten years earlier.

19.
Tatra 87 1947

THE TATRA COMPANY, NAMED FOR THE HIGHEST RANGE OF THE CARPATHIAN Mountains, came into being in 1920. Tatra was in fact the new name for Nesselsdorfer, the automobile company founded in 1897 in the former Austro-Hungarian Empire.

The first Nesselsdorfer, the *Präsident*, was developed by a small group of engineers that included Edmund Rumpler and a young man by the name of Hans Ledwinka.

Rumpler soon left the firm, but Ledwinka became its director and guiding light. In the 1920s, he developed a series of passenger and racing cars for the company, renamed Tatra and now situated in the new republic of Czechoslovakia created as a result of the postwar redrawing of the European map. Ledwinka's main claim to fame, however, would be the Tatra models developed after 1934. The Tatra 87 and its predecessor, the 77, were based on two fundamental principles: an aerodynamic body style inspired by the work of Paul Jaray[1] and a rear-mounted engine. The rationale for this placement of the motor was that it would eliminate the cumbersome driveshaft, reduce noise and provide a roomier passenger compartment.[2]

The all-steel bodywork of the 87, launched in 1937, covered a monocoque chassis. The sedan had a rounded front hood covering the trunk, no grille, and a third, central headlight. The very wide, one-piece windscreen was flanked by small vertical windows. The rounded back had one tiny, rectangular window, while the engine cover had a single protruding fin to maximize air flow. Large lateral air intakes on the rear side panels cooled the engine, taking the place of the single scoop right across the engine cover that had replaced the rear window on the Tatra 77. Like the 77, the 87 had "suicide" doors in the front.

The rear-mounted, air-cooled V8 was integrated with the clutch, transmission and differential. Its two rows of pistons were set at 90°, and its displacement was 3 litres, compared to the 77's 3.4-litre V8. Despite this small reduction, the 87's motor was in fact a bit more powerful, at 73 hp compared to the earlier model's 70 hp.

The Tatra 87 had a four-wheel independent suspension and four drum brakes. The concentration of weight in the rear resulted in a

Tatra 87 1947

ENGINE

Type: V8, with overhead valves, air-cooled. Displacement: 3,969 cc. Bore and stroke: 75 mm x 84 mm. Horsepower: 72 hp at 3,600 rpm[3]

DIMENSIONS

Length: 4,740 mm; width: 1,670 mm; height: 1,500mm; wheelbase: 2,850 mm; weight: 1,370 kg

TRANSMISSION

4-speed manual

PERFORMANCE

Maximum speed: 160 km/h

COLLECTION

Walter Baran collection, Ashland, Pennsylvania

1   Setright 1976, p. 59.

2   Tatra/De Dubé 1969, p. 311.

3   Rogliatti 1971, p. 113.

tendency to oversteer that demanded a lot of attention from the driver. During World War II, several serious accidents prompted the High Command of the occupying German Army to prohibit its officers from driving these Tatras.

Following the war, the new socialist state of Czechoslovakia nationalized the Tatra company; Ledwinka was imprisoned for six years and then forced into exile. Tatra continued to produce mainly the heavy trucks and railroad equipment needed for postwar reconstruction. In 1949, production of the 87 was stopped. It was replaced by the Tatraplan, a more developed model that Ledwinka had in fact designed during the war.

20.

Auto-Union D V12 1938

AUTO-UNION, WITH ITS SYMBOL OF FOUR INTER-LINKED RINGS, WAS THE NAME given to a consortium of four German automakers of the early 1930s: Audi, Horch, DKW and Wanderer. The name was also used for Ferdinand Porsche's famous *P-Wagen* Grand Prix single-seaters.

In the summer of 1933, Auto-Union began working on a revolutionary new design for a Grand Prix racer. The car was to have a rear-mounted, supercharged V16 engine and a four-wheel independent suspension. The engine would be mounted between the rear axle and the gas tank. From 1934 to 1937, the engine's displacement grew from 4.35 litres (Auto-Union A) to 4.95 litres (B) to 6.0 litres (C). The tubular chassis also served for the engine cooling system, with some coolant pipes passing through the chassis tubes. The front suspension used half axles and torsion bars, while the rear suspension was equipped with double wishbones combined with transversal leaf springs.

Auto-Union cars were nicknamed "Silver Arrows" because of their silver gray bodies. (Like its competitors, Mercedes, the company chose the national colour used by Germany on the Grand Prix circuit.) The Auto-Union racers proved particularly effective on fast circuits but, on more winding tracks, their drivers were obliged to use particular care because of the cars' pronounced oversteer.

The *P-Wagen* first appeared on Berlin's Avus track in March 1934. Driver Hans Stuck immediately set three world speed records. From 1934 to 1939, *P-Wagens* won 24 of the 61 Grand Prix races in which they took part.

In 1938, Porsche left the project to put all his time into Hitler's "people's car." Leadership of the *P-Wagen* project went to Porsche's assistant, Professor Robert Eberan von Eberhorst.[1] That same year, Grand Prix rules changed, leading Eberhorst to replace the V16 engine with a supercharged V12.

Named the Typ D, the 1938 Auto-Union had an engine with triple camshafts. The central shaft controlled the intake valves, while the others (one for each row of cylinders, which were set at 60°) controlled the exhaust valves. Engine displacement was reduced to

---

Auto-Union D V12 1938

ENGINE
Type: V12, with 24 valves. Displacement: 2,984 cc. Bore and stroke: 65 mm x 75 mm. Horsepower: 485-500 hp at 7,000 rpm

DIMENSIONS:
Length: 4,420 mm; width: 1,720 mm; height: 1,080 mm; wheelbase: 2,896 mm; weight: 850 kg

TRANSMISSION:
5-speed manual

PERFORMANCE:
Maximum speed: 330 km/h

COLLECTION:
Barbara and Paul Karassik

---

1   Auto-Union/Merlin 1981, p. 13.

3.0 litres while, for the suspension, Eberhorst adopted a DeDion rear axle with torsion bars.

The V12 engine, which originally provided 420 hp, had its power increased to 485 hp in 1939 when the original supercharger was replaced by a Roots double-phase supercharger.[2] Eberhorst also installed a smaller, 200-litre fuel tank, along with twin 40-litre tanks for mixing methanol and benzol. These two tanks were placed on either side of the driver. This new arrangement improved weight distribution and allowed the cockpit to be mounted further back.

Getting the Typ D into operation took longer than expected, however. The car missed the first three 1938 Grand Prix races, and its racing debut was a disappointment. Nonetheless, the V12 Auto-Union was victorious in several Grand Prix in 1938 and 1939, including those in England, Rumania, France and Yugoslavia. The great Italian driver, Tazio Nuvolari, won this last Grand Prix on the very day that France and Great Britain declared war on Germany.

This Typ D Auto-Union is the only original *P-Wagen* still in existence. It was discovered in the Soviet Union after World War II and was restored at the end of the 1970s, when it was fitted with a 485-hp engine. It is interesting to note that, some 50 years after the appearance of the *P-Wagen*, all Formula I racing stables have adopted a tubular chassis, rear engine and four-wheel independent suspension.

2   Casucci 1981, p. 54.

21.

Bentley 4 1/4-Litre Embiricos 1938

THE BENTLEY 4 1/4-LITRE WAS LAUNCHED IN 1936. IT WAS THE FIRST automobile produced under the Bentley name after the departure of the company's founder, Walter Owen Bentley. Following the takeover of Bentley Motors by Rolls-Royce in 1931, the Bentley had become no more than "a Rolls with a Bentley grille." The decision to use the 4 1/4-litre engine, designed for the Rolls-Royce 25/30, simply confirmed this fact.

Bentley 4 1/4-Litre Embiricos 1938

ENGINE
Type: straight 6, two SU carburetors. Displacement: 4,255 cc. Bore and stroke: 89 mm x 114 mm. Horsepower: 140 hp[3]

DIMENSIONS
Length: 5,180 mm; width: 1,980 mm; height: not provided; wheelbase: 3,200 mm; weight: not provided

TRANSMISSION
4-speed manual

PERFORMANCE
Maximum speed: 195 km/h[4]

COLLECTION
Arturo Keller Collection, Petaluma, California

The straight 6-cylinder engine provided 126-hp, enabling these cars to reach a speed of 160 km/h. Company publicity maintained that the new 4 1/4-litre engine was designed especially for users of high-speed roads "like the *autobahn* and the *autostrada*."

In 1938, the head of Franco-Britannic Autos de Paris, which was the French importer of Rolls-Royce and Bentley, received an order from A. M. Embiricos, a young Greek shipping magnate who lived in Paris. A fan of fast cars, the Paris resident was looking for a streamlined 2+2 automobile capable of high speeds.

French designer Georges Paulin drew up sketches for a coupe. He replaced the traditional Bentley grille with a curved one that was flanked by headlights set inside the fenders. The windshield was V-shaped.

The resulting Embiricos, with a light alloy body by Pourtout, weighed 90 kg less than a standard Bentley 4 1/4-litre.[1]

To make the most of the car's engine, its compression ratio was increased and the original carburetors were replaced by larger-capacity SU models, boosting the engine's output to 140 hp.

This aerodynamic Bentley was delivered to its owner in July 1938. Factory personnel had heard rumours about the vehicle and asked to have a closer look. In January 1939, a three-day test in France and Germany gave company employees an opportunity to discover the new model's potential. Since the British company had taken care to publicize the event, it was soon approached by other buyers interested in owning an automobile like the Embiricos.[2]

1 Bentley/Posthumus 1983, not paginated.

2 Kimes (ed.) 1976, p. 170.

3 Bentley/Posthumus.

4 Ibid.

A year later, the well-known British driver, George Eyston, at the wheel of the same car, achieved an average speed of 185.15 km/h over a distance of 16.09 km at the Brooklands track in England. Shortly afterwards, the Embiricos was purchased by H. F. S. Hay. After World War II, it would make three appearances in the Le Mans 24-hour race, the first time in 1949, when it ran sixth.[5] After the 1950 and 1951 races, however, the car's team (J. Hay and T. H. Wisdom) was obliged to face the obvious: their car had aged substantially compared with the competition.

5   Bentley/Adams and Roberts 1978, p. 157.

22.

BMW 328 1938

THE BMW 328 GOT OFF TO A PROMISING START. ON JUNE 14, 1936, driver Ernst Henne won the Eifelrennen race completing the 114-km course at an average speed of 101 km/h. The astonished crowd had just witnessed the birth of the 328.

Production of this new sports car began in February 1937. A two-seater, the 328 used a more advanced version of the same in-line 6-cylinder engine found in earlier BMW models (the 315, 319, etc.). The last BMW to use a tubular chassis, it had the same wheelbase and track, both front and rear, as previous models. The independent front suspension and the transversal leaf spring attached to the rear axle assembly had also undergone little modification.

On the other hand, the 328 came equipped with new hydraulic brakes, a recent innovation from the Munich manufacturer. The system provided more balanced and progressive braking than its rivals.

The 2.0-litre, 80-hp engine provided ample power to propel the 830-kg convertible to 100 km/h in less than 11 seconds. Maximum speed was about 150 km/h.

The 328's efficient streamlined silhouette was marked by headlights set down between the fenders and the bean-shaped twin grilles that were typical of BMWs since the 1933 303 model. The car had solid disk wheels, hidden in the rear by standard wheel covers. The spare wheel was stored in the roof of the trunk, a feature included on the 328 despite the car's obvious sports appeal.

The two occupants sat in a relatively spacious and well appointed cockpit that even sported a glove box.

The 328 was often victorious on the racing circuit. Its triumphs included the *Mille Miglia* held after the outbreak of World War II in 1940.

Following the war, the 328's 2.0-litre engine provided the mechanical basis for cars manufactured by Fraser-Nash and Bristol in England, and by Veritas in Germany.

In 1936, only two 328s were built; both were designed for racing. From 1937 to 1940, a total of 460 were manufactured, most as elegant convertibles. BMW also delivered chassis for 59 more cars,

BMW 328 1938

ENGINE
Type: in-line 6, with overhead valves, 3 Solex carburetors.
Displacement: 1,971 cc. Bore and stroke: 66 mm x 96 mm.
Horsepower: 80 hp at 5,000 rpm

DIMENSIONS
Length: 3,900 mm; width: 1,550 mm; height: 1,118 mm;
wheelbase: 2,400 mm; weight: 830 kg

TRANSMISSION
4-speed manual

PERFORMANCE
Maximum speed: 150 km/h.[1]
Acceleration: 0 to 100 km/h in 10.4 seconds[2]

COLLECTION
Rosso Bianco Collection, Aschaffenburg, Germany

---

1 BMW/Schrader 1979, p. 159.

2 BMW/Norbye 1984, p. 66.

the bodies of which would come from other workshops.[3] It is estimated that about 150 of these cars are still in existence.

The popularity of the 328 has endured over the years; even today it has its loyal fans. Some coachbuilders, like Franco Sbarro of Switzerland, have even produced relatively precise reproductions of the 328, which are available to today's buyers.

3   BMW/Simsa 1984, p. 159

23.

Bowes Seal Fast Special 1938-1939

IN 1937, AMERICAN LOUIS MEYER DROVE THE INDIANAPOLIS 500 FOR THE eleventh time. At 33, Meyer already had over a dozen years of motor racing under his belt, and this time he was driving the Indy for the Boyle Products company.

The Boyle car was fitted with a modernized version of an 8-cylinder Miller engine, and Meyer drove it to a fourth-place finish. The next year, Meyer would again drive a Miller engine-equipped vehicle, but this time car number five bore the name of a different sponsor: Bowes Seal Fast.

The shape of Indy one-seaters had changed a lot since the heroic days of the Miller 91. They were both longer and higher, and increasingly extensive bodies hid most of the undercarriage. Streamlining to reduce wind resistance was increasingly evident.

Louis Meyer's own automobile was an amalgam of different parts. Meyer himself had built the chassis and some of the mechanical components. Fred Offenhauser, a well-known Indy engine specialist, had made some engine parts, including the block. The body work had been done by Myron Stevens and Phil Summers.

It was May 30, 1938, when Meyer started his twelfth Indy 500. He had qualified twelfth out of a field of 33.[1] Unfortunately, his oil pump broke on the 149th lap, when he was in fourth place, and he was obliged to withdraw from the race.

In 1939, he tried again, still driving the Bowes Seal Fast Special. The chassis was unchanged, but the 8-cylinder engine had been equipped with a supercharger by engine specialist Windfield, with a resulting increase of 100 hp.[2]

Bowes Seal Fast Special 1938-1939

ENGINE
Type: in-line 8 cylinder. Displacement: 2,934 cc. Bore and stroke: not provided. Horsepower: not provided

DIMENSIONS
Length: 3,990 mm; width: 1,850 mm; height, wheelbase and weight: not provided

TRANSMISSION
4-speed manual

PERFORMANCE
Maximum speed: 208 km/h

COLLECTION
Indianapolis Motor Speedway Hall of Fame Museum, Indianapolis

When the time came to qualify, Meyer beat the Indy record with a speed of 208.107 km/h. Unfortunately, another driver had managed to beat him at 208.221 km/h. From his second spot on the starting line, Meyer secretly hoped to take his fourth Indy 500 victory. In third position, however, was the great Wilbur Shaw; driving a powerful Boyle-Maserati, he promised some tough competition.

From the start Meyer set a gruelling pace, quickly pulling in front. Only Shaw seemed capable of keeping up with him. Meyer

---

1   Miller/*500-Mile Race Record Book* 1980, p. 42.

2   Bowes/*Automobile Quarterly* 1994, pp. 74-75.

remained in first place for the first 400 laps, but then Shaw made his push for first. A fierce struggle ensued between the two frontrunners. Just three laps from the finish,[3] Meyer hit a patch of oil and lost control. The Bowes skidded, Meyer was thrown free, and Wilbur Shaw won the twentieth running of the Indianapolis 500.

Louis Meyer's thirteenth try for the Indy 500 could easily have cost him his life. Remarkably, he walked away unhurt, but the accident led him to put an end to his racing career.

3   Miller/500-Mile Race Record Book 1980, p. 42.

24.

Bugatti 57 Atlantic 1938

THE 57 ATLANTIC WAS UNQUESTIONABLY JEAN BUGATTI'S MASTERPIECE. A sculpture on wheels, a mixture of shapes quickly sketched, it simultaneously obeyed the twin dictates of motion and aerodynamics.

Jean Bugatti showed the new design for the first time at the 1935 Salon de Paris. The Bugatti Aérolithe, built on a Type 57 chassis, caused a sensation. Even the trunk, set in the rounded, rear section of the body, had a circular lid.

To lighten the vehicle, Jean Bugatti chose to build the body of Elektron, a magnesium-aluminum alloy made by a German company. Although very light, the alloy was difficult to stamp and to weld. The solution was to rivet in place the passenger compartment panels and the front and rear fenders. This resulted in ridges like those found on aircraft of the day. The 2-seater had a definite spaceship look about it, and Buck Rogers would surely have driven an Aérolithe... had he been French.

The unusual headlights were set into the inner sides of the fenders and mounted low, where a bumper would normally be found. By contrast, the flat radiator, which was taken from a stock model, seemed to contradict the rounded forms of the body. A compromise, the radiator came from a production model 57; it forced a high belt line, so high that access to the passenger compartment was particularly difficult.

To compensate for the high sill, which was evident when the "suicide" doors were open, Bugatti set the doors high into the roof. As for the rear wheels, they were so completely streamlined that no more than a fifth of them could be seen. Lastly, the Aérolithe had no windshield wipers.

In 1936, Jean Bugatti proposed an "improved" version of the car. He renamed it the Atlantic and built it on a lowered Type 57S or 57SC chassis with an 8-cylinder engine that produced 170 hp, or 200 hp when equipped with an optional supercharger. The Atlantic had windshield wipers, and its larger headlights were more prominent than its predeccessors'. The flat radiator had, fortunately,

Bugatti 57 Atlantic 1938

ENGINE
Type: straight 8, with or without supercharger
Displacement: 3,257 cc. Bore and stroke: 72 mm x 100 mm.
Horsepower: 170/200 hp at 5,500 rpm
DIMENSIONS
Length: 4,470 mm; width: 1,727 mm; height: 1,295 mm;
wheelbase: 2,972 mm; weight: 953 kg
TRANSMISSION
4-speed manual
PERFORMANCE
Maximum speed: 200 km/h[1]
COLLECTION
Ralph Lauren Collection

1   Bugatti/Sauzay 1990, p. 84.

been replaced by a V-shape version. This radiator had an elegant frame and was ornamented with a pointed design suggestive of motion. Thanks to the lowered chassis, the hood was no higher than the fenders, which added to its spectacular appearance. The car itself was no higher than 1.3 metres.

According to historian Maurice Sauzay, the first two Atlantics were built in 1936. The first was delivered to an American, via England, in September of the same year. The second went to a French customer in October. The third, which is the one seen here, went to a Londoner named Pope in May 1938.[2] Surprising though it may seem, all three cars have survived to the present day!

The Atlantic was undoubtedly the most impressive of the Type 57 automobiles, which were in turn the most popular Bugattis ever built. Between 1934 and 1939, the Molsheim works turned out almost 700 of the various versions of the Type 57.

2   Bugatti/Conway and Sauzay 1989, p. 110.

25.

Dubonnet Xenia 1938-1946

THE HISTORY OF THE DUBONNET XENIA IS UNIQUE. IT BEGAN WITH ANDRÉ Dubonnet, grandson of Jean Dubonnet who, in 1846, created "an original-tasting aperitif for his family and friends"[1] and became a tycoon of the wine industry. An enthusiastic sportsman like his father Marius, André Dubonnet began with a passion for military aviation, moved on to road and boat racing, and then devoted himself – and his fortune – to his real love, the automobile.

No more than four or five automobiles bearing the Dubonnet name were ever built, along with a few demonstration chassis. The Dubonnets were devotees of Hispano-Suiza – they purchased at least a dozen over 15 years[2] – and the first Dubonnet, a Targa two-seater, would be built by Nieuport. André used it in a race in Sicily in 1924.

André was particularly interested in modern techniques. Towards the end of the 1920s, he met French engineer Gustave Chedru. Although recently retired, Chedru had an idea for a revolutionary suspension, but he lacked a financial backer. The two men's collaboration led to the birth of an independent suspension system that would later be purchased by the American General Motors Corporation. The system would be called the "Dubonnet suspension." Starting in 1934, the Dubonnet system, renamed the "Knee-Action Suspension", was used by GM on Chevrolets and Pontiacs.

A few chassis were constructed to test the suspension. At the 1932 Paris Auto Show, the first Xenia was unveiled: a 4-door sedan equipped with a fixed roof, front-wheel drive and the new Dubonnet suspension. On the hood, a plaque bore the symbol André Dubonnet had proposed for the marque: a leaping cat, to suggest the effectiveness of the new suspension. The extremely angular forms of the Xenia were in marked contrast to the streamlined car with retractable headlights that Dubonnet had promised.

Why "Xenia"? The name was devised simply to capture public attention and curiosity, and was a pure exercise in marketing.

Dubonnet Xenia 1938-1946

ENGINE
Type: straight 6 Hispano-Suiza H6C, OHC. Displacement: 7,983 cc.
Bore and stroke: 100 mm x 140 mm. Horsepower: 160 hp at 3,000 rpm

DIMENSIONS
Length: 5,700 mm; width: 2,000 mm; height: not provided; wheelbase: 3,710 mm; weight: 1,800 kg

TRANSMISSION
3-speed manual

PERFORMANCE
Maximum speed: 200 km/h[3]

COLLECTION
Private collection

1 Dubonnet/Usher 1986, p. 274.

2 Ibid., p. 275.

3 Dubonnet/Thevenet n. d. , p. 70.

Just prior to World War II, Dubonnet asked Saoutchic, the Parisian coachbuilder, to build a sports coupe to his specifications. This long automobile probably used the same Hispano engine found in the first Xenia, but this time the car's streamlined appearance symbolized speed, and the driving wheels were in the rear.

The two sliding doors were mounted on parallelogram hinges. Overall, the coupe looked somewhat like a fast airplane. The greatly streamlined front end had integrated headlights, while the extremely rounded windshield was made of a single piece of glass that brought to mind a cockpit. The rear wheels were hidden behind fender skirts and the "ducktail" rear end resembled the prototype Peugeot NX4, built by French engineer Andreau and shown at the 1936 Paris Auto show.

This second Xenia was essentially a very personal gift from André Dubonnet to himself. He nonetheless hoped to use it to set new speed records. Perhaps this is why some automotive historians maintain that the car was equipped with a V12 Hispano engine. Today the Xenia has a 6-cylinder engine from a Hispano-Suiza H6C. Whatever the case, World War II put an end to Dubonnet's sporting ambitions. Although it is thought that the Xenia could reach 200 km/h, its only public performance occurred in 1946, when it inaugurated the Saint Cloud Tunnel at the start of the great Normandy autoroute.

26.

Talbot-Lago T150 SS 1938

HISTORY WILL FOREVER ASSOCIATE THE NAMES TALBOT-LAGO, FIGONI AND Falaschi with one of the most beautiful automotive creations the world has ever seen. The Talbot-Lago T150 SS stands as a jewel among automobiles, as admired today as in the past. It was a perfect expression of the splendour of 1930s high society, but the coupe's simple lines have withstood the test of time.

The teardrop shape so dear to aerodynamicists in the 1930s reached its ultimate expression in this two-door sedan. Comparisons with Jean Bugatti's 1934 Atalante are inevitable. The clean, unbroken lines designed by Figoni and Falaschi create an aesthetic balance that is also remarkable.

The T150 SS was innovative in more ways than one. It sported a two-piece windscreen, that was sharply raked for the period, oval side windows and grille – Jaguar would later use this oval motif – pontoon-shaped rear fenders, and fine vertical grilles that hid its radiator and headlights. Chrome was everywhere: in the front, chrome accentuated the curves of the body, while in the rear, chrome trim that began under the rear window fanned down along the sides to accentuate the fluid effect of the car's lines.

The T150's interior exhibited a similar degree of luxury. The two occupants sat on seats of the same high-grade supple leather that lined the two doors. The window frames were of the same fine wood as the dashboard, where circular Jaeger dials displayed the car's speed, rpms, temperature and oil pressure.

The wooden, four-spoke steering wheel, with its small indentations to provide a better grip, gave the driver a sense of being at one with the car. The 4.0-litre, in-line 6-cylinder engine provided power ranging from 140 to 165 hp, depending on the model.

The T150 was unveiled to a delighted public at the 1937 Paris Auto Show, but fewer than 20 units would be produced before 1939. Although each T150 SS was built to order, the cars varied little one from another. According to the most optimistic estimates, no more than a quarter of these automobiles have survived.

Talbot-Lago T150 SS 1938

ENGINE
Type: in-line 6, with overhead valves, 2 Zenith carburetors.
Displacement: 3,998 cc. Bore and stroke: 90 mm x 104.5 mm.
Horsepower: 160 hp at 4,100 rpm

DIMENSIONS
Length: 4,300 mm; width: 1,670 mm; height: not provided;
wheelbase: 2,642 mm; weight: 1,400 kg

TRANSMISSION
4-speed Wilson with pre-selector

PERFORMANCE
Maximum speed: 175 km/h

COLLECTION
Rosso Bianco Collection, Aschaffenburg, Germany

The T150 SS showed the future of automobile design: the gradual merging of the fenders into the body, the round lines, the rake of the windshield, the elimination of the running board, etc.

The Talbot-Lago name was borne by French automobiles built by Automobiles Talbot SA of Suresnes[1] between 1934 and 1959. Anthony Lago had been sent to the Suresnes factory to take charge of the French division of the Franco-British consortium Sunbeam-Talbot-Darracq (STD). He regained control after the consortium collapsed in 1935. To relaunch the Talbot name, he backed a return

1   Aceti 1979, p. 40.

to sports car production but also proposed that renowned designers, including Figoni and Falaschi, provide some chassis with luxurious coachwork. Incidentally, Talbots destined for the British market were sold under the Darracq name until 1939.

27.

Bugatti 64 Coach 1939

SOME HISTORIANS FEEL THAT BUGATTI WAS SLOW TO DEVELOP NOT ONLY because of the Depression but also because of Ettore Bugatti's obstinate refusal to adopt modern technical solutions. Jean Bugatti, son of "le Patron," took a more progressive view. On more than one occasion he had attempted to convince his father of the need to modernize the cars coming out of Bugatti's Molsheim works. Had it not been for Jean's untimely death in 1939, the 64 would have served to demonstrate the point.

This sedan was intended to replace the 57, a popular Bugatti launched at the Salon de Paris in 1933. Built under Jean's supervision, the 57 retained traditional Ettore features, including its one-piece, rigid front axle and cable-operated brakes. The 57 was produced for six years, right up to the outbreak of World War II, and some 630 of them were manufactured.

Work on the Type 64 began in 1938, and was completed in 1939. The 57's successor had a 4.4-litre aluminum engine with nine bearings, developed from the motor used in the 50B, but without a supercharger. Fuel was provided through a carburetor. The top speed attributed to the car was between 175 and 200 km/h, a very impressive performance for the end of the 1930s. The 64 was also to use hydraulic brakes on all four wheels, a feature used for the first time on the 57 in 1938.

The development of the 64 coincided with Jean Bugatti's arrival as factory director, which no doubt explains the 64's Cotal gearbox with electromagnetic preselector, the duralumin chassis and the hydraulic brakes.

The 64's body confirmed the genius of Ettore Bugatti's son. Jean had designed a two-door sedan with particularly modern and fluid lines, smooth, without projections. His innovative spirit was evident in the design of the side windows, which were flush with the body panels, a practice only recently adopted in most contemporary automobiles. In addition, doors that extended into the roof provided easier access.

The hybrid style of the 64 retained some characteristics of the 57 Galibier four-door sedan, in particular the front fenders and the curved roof. It also borrowed the oval radiator, two-piece windshield

Bugatti 64 Coach 1939

ENGINE
Type: in-line 8, DOHC, 2 valves per cylinder. Displacement: 4,432 cc. Bore and stroke: 84 mm x 100 mm. Power: 185 hp at 5,000 rpm

DIMENSIONS
Length: 5,300 mm; width: 1,800 mm; height: not provided; wheelbase: 3,300 mm; weight: 1,265 kg

TRANSMISSION
Cotal 4-speed

PERFORMANCE
Maximum speed: 175 - 200 km/h

COLLECTION
Musée national de l'Automobile de Mulhouse, France, Schlump Collection

and "artillery shell" headlights of the 57C Atlantic coupe, a strange throwback compared to the Galibier, whose lights were built into the front fenders.

Tragically, on August 11, 1939, Jean Bugatti died while testing a racing Bugatti. The accident occurred when the younger Bugatti, driving at 220 km/h on a closed public highway near the company plant in Alsace, was startled by the sudden appearance of a cyclist. Disillusioned by the death of his 30-year-old son, Ettore Bugatti spent the last years of his life trying to envision the automobile that France would need following the war. The 64 was never produced.

28.

Lagonda Le Mans Lancefield V12 1939

In 1933, ROLLS-ROYCE ACQUIRED BENTLEY MOTORS. THE BENTLEY company's founder, Walter Owen Bentley, found himself relegated to secondary tasks and after two years quit Rolls-Royce to become technical director at Lagonda.

Many experts believe that Bentley created his masterwork for Lagonda: a 4.5-litre, V12 engine. Presented at the 1937 London Motor Show, the engine enabled Lagonda to offer prestige vehicles that could compete with Rolls-Royce, whose Phantom III came with a 7.3-litre V12.

Bentley's V12 had a chain-driven camshaft for each row of cylinders, which were angled at 60°. The commercial version produced 180 hp[1] and was redlined at about 5,500 rpm. This gave a driver enough flexibility to accelerate from 7 to 103.45 mph in third gear without faltering.[2]

Lagondas had been active on the sports circuit from the early 1930s. In 1935, a Lagonda piloted by the team of Hindmarsh and Fontés won the Le Mans 24-hour race. The following year, however, a strike cancelled the event, and in 1937, mechanical problems forced Hindmarsh to withdraw after only a few circuits.

In any case, a simpler mechanical arrangement was needed to compete with Alfa-Romeo, and Bentley's V12 seemed a promising avenue. The company decided to produce two cars for the 1939 Le Mans race. Usually Lagonda built its own bodies, but in this case it called upon the London coachbuilder Lancefield, active in the field since 1921. (After 1948, Lancefield would concentrate solely on aircraft components.)

Lancefield's designers came up with a streamlined body equipped with a large window area (unusual for aerodynamically designed automobiles of the 1930s). "Teardrop" front fenders accentuated the look, although this was contradicted somewhat by the massive radiator grille. The Lancefield body had neither the bumpers nor the running boards found on the stock Lagonda Rapide, but the coachbuilder did retain the marque's characteristic mudguard on the front portion of the rear fender.

Lagonda Le Mans Lancefield V12 1939

ENGINE
Type: V12, with side-valves and Polyrhoe carburetor. Displacement: 4,480 cc. Bore and stroke: 75 mm x 84.5 mm. Horsepower: 225 hp

DIMENSIONS
Length: 4,850 mm; width: 1,900 mm; height, wheelbase and weight: not provided

TRANSMISSION
4-speed manual

PERFORMANCE
Maximum speed: 177 km/h[3]

COLLECTION
Rosso Bianco Collection, Aschaffenburg, Germany

1 Vanderveen ed. 1973, p. 73.

2 Georgano ed. 1973, p. 413.

3 Culshaw and Horrobin 1974, p. 194.

Lancefield also produced streamlined one-seaters that resembled transformed Lagonda Rapide roadsters. The bodies of these racing monsters were light and very narrow, providing just enough space for the driver and revealing the perforated side rails of the chassis. Short fenders acted as mudguards, covering the wheels. The tiny windshield was framed by a spoiler of sorts that surrounded the driver. The shape was simple but extremely effective.

Motor sports historian Michael Cotton believes that W. O. Bentley did not really want to see the two cars on the starting line at Le Mans.[4] Perhaps he feared that they would not match the exploits of the 1920s, when Blower Bentleys took the honours at Le Mans five times. Whatever the case, by the time the endurance test was over, the effectiveness of Bentley's V12 was proven. The streamlined Lagondas piloted by the teams of Dobson/Brackenbury and Seldson/Waleran had come third and fourth. This achievement led to expectations of a Lagonda victory at the 1940 Le Mans, but within three months Europe was at war.

Following the war, the 4.5-litre V12 was shelved. One of the two single-seaters would be destroyed in an absolute speed test. The other would end up in the Rosso Bianco Collection. Bentley himself perfected a 2.5-litre 6-cylinder engine to be used in a new range of sedans. In 1947, British businessman David Brown purchased Lagonda and merged it with Aston-Martin. Shortly afterwards, W. O. Bentley resigned to move on to Armstrong-Siddeley.

4   Cotton 1989, p. 37.

29.

Mercedes-Benz 320 1939

THE SECOND HALF OF THE 1930S SAW THE APPEARANCE OF A HOST OF automobiles whose fluid forms were the result of research in aerodynamics. Although the stated purpose of such rounded body designs was that they enable the automobile to better "cut through" the air, car manufacturers were also fully aware of the advertising value of these exotic vehicles. As proof of this, they had merely to observe the crowds who came out to look at the automobiles.

With the building of the *autobahn*, Hitler's Germany had embarked on an enormous highway construction project. The government also heavily subsidized aeronautics research. These factors together had stimulated auto-makers to construct streamlined automobiles.

Naturally, the coupe design was particularly amenable to aerodynamic principles, since its shorter rear section made streamlining easier. The amazing Mercedes-Benz 500K illustrates the point. The *Autobahn-Kurier*, as it was known, was launched in 1934. It was characterized by a long, arched hood, streamlined rear wheels and a two-door passenger compartment whose profile described a gentle, continuous curve all the way from the windshield to the lower rear of the car.

Mercedes-Benz 320 1939
ENGINE
Type: straight 6. Displacement: 3,405 cc.
Bore and stroke: 85 mm x 100 mm. Horsepower: 78 hp
DIMENSIONS
Length: 5,350 mm; width: 1,850 mm; height: 1,650 mm;
wheelbase: not provided; weight: 2,000 kg
TRANSMISSION
4-speed manual
PERFORMANCE
Maximum speed: 125 km/h
COLLECTION
Mercedes-Benz-Museum, Stuttgart

The application of this aesthetic approach to mass-produced sedans (such as the American Chrysler Airflow, the Czech Tatra Type 87 and the French Panhard Dynamic) would take longer, since buyers were not yet prepared for the change in established values implied by the new designs. The new, aerodynamic approach was therefore seen first on luxury sedans and on some limousines.

The Mercedes-Benz 320 streamlined sedan exemplifies this approach. Built at the Mercedes Mannheim plant, it went on the market in 1939. Its elongated form recalled the 500K *Autobahn-Kurier*; it was as if the coupe had been transformed into the longer sedan. The streamlined 320 did in fact use a long-wheelbase chassis.

The 320 had first appeared in the Mercedes line-up in 1936, and had first been offered as a conventional sedan, a Pullman limousine, a torpedo, a convertible and a roadster. Until 1938, it was equipped with a 3.2-litre, 6-cylinder engine. In 1939, Mercedes began

commercial production of the 320 and increased it's engine displacement to 3.4-litres.

From 1936 to 1939, Mercedes built slightly more than 4,000 320s. The streamlined sedans found few buyers, however. Not only were they expensive but the public still saw their strange shape as little more than an exuberant stylistic exercise. In those days, drivers were not overly concerned with the Cd rating of their automobiles.

30

Chrysler Newport Dual Cowl Phaeton 1941

BARELY SIX YEARS AFTER LAUNCHING THE FAMOUS BUT UNPOPULAR AIRFLOW, Chrysler Corporation unveiled two show cars that were almost as eccentric in appearance: the Newport and the Thunderbolt.

Like the 1938 Buick Y-Job, the two cars were to act as mobile market research laboratories that could be used to evaluate the public taste in design.

Until then, American manufacturers had been wary of presenting new ideas in the public arena before production vehicles were actually available. They feared that the anticipation might lead to a drop in sales. With the Newport and the Thunderbolt, the reverse was true.

Starting in the fall of 1940, a dozen prototypes – six of each car – were produced and then shown at auto shows and major dealers around the country. The new 1941 models became available at the same time. Rather than draw attention away from Chrysler's regular models, the Newport and the Thunderbolt in fact increased demand for the company's cars.

Pure stylistic exercises, the two cars used mechanical components from existing production models. The Newport was built on a 1941 Chrysler Imperial chassis, while the Thunderbolt used a New Yorker chassis. The bodywork was created by LeBaron of Detroit, which had been making special bodies for Chrysler for many years. Ralph Roberts designed the Newport, while the Thunderbolt sprung from the imagination of Alex Tremulis who, after the war, would design the body for the Tucker.

Roberts described the Newport as a modern version of the dual cowl phaetons of the 1920s and 1930s. The car's long, enveloping coachwork was made of aluminum. It had dual passenger compartments, each with its own windshield. A push-button mechanism opened the doors, while the convertible roof, hidden under a panel behind the rear seat, was operated hydraulically.

Contradicting current trends, the Newport sported little chrome. Like the Cord 810/812, which ceased production in 1937, the car had retractable headlights.

Chrysler Newport Dual Cowl Phaeton 1941

ENGINE
Type: in-line 8 Cadillac, Stromberg carburetor.
Displacement: 5,303 cc. Bore and stroke: 82.5 mm x 123.8 mm.
Horsepower: 140 hp at 3,400 rpm[1]
DIMENSIONS
Length: 5,690 mm; width: 1,651 mm; height: 1,499 mm;
wheelbase: 3,683 mm; weight: 2,231 kg
TRANSMISSION
3-speed manual
PERFORMANCE
Maximum speed: not provided
COLLECTION
The William F. Harrah Foundation National Automobile Museum, Reno, Nevada

---

1   Kimes and Clark 1985, p. 302.

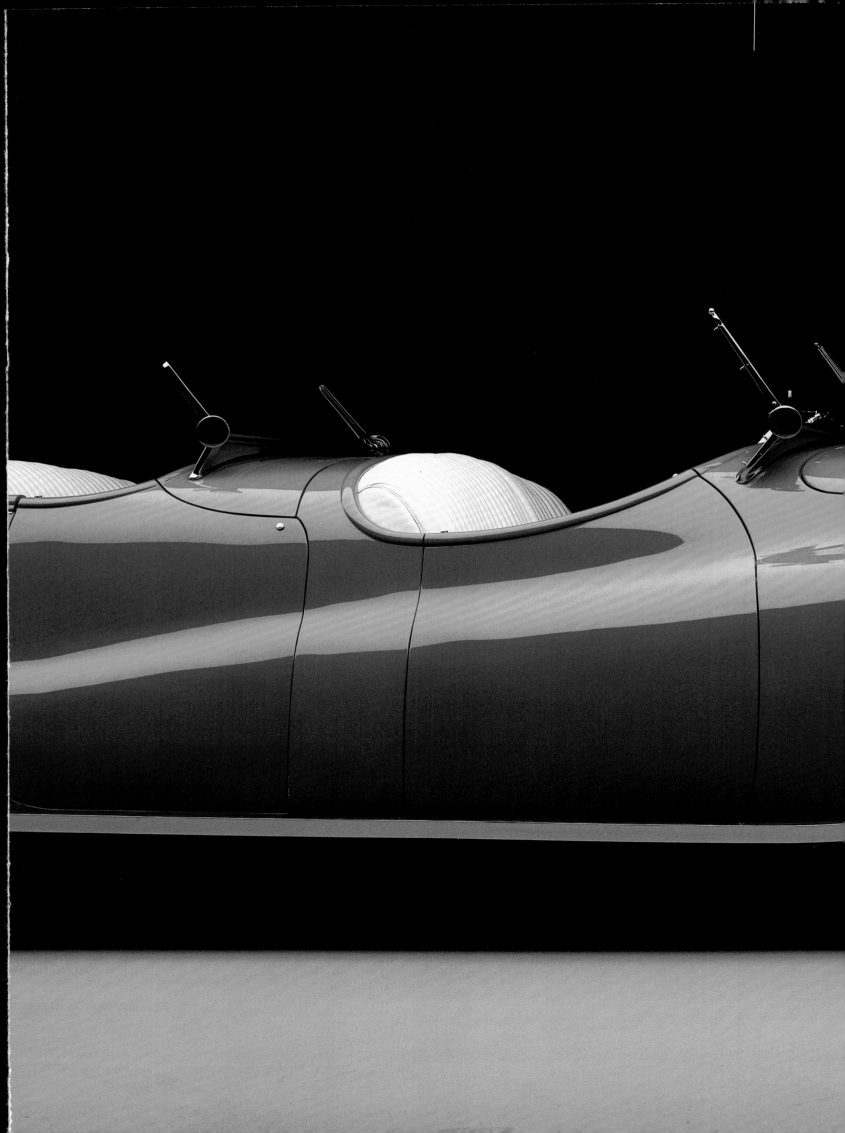

For 1941, however, the Newport was an anachronism. The era of the chauffeur-driven limousine was over, so the Newport was useful only for parades or for transporting dignitaries. One of the Newports was in fact used as the pace car at the 1941 Indianapolis 500.

The Thunderbolt was more modest. A two-seater with a rigid, removable roof, it resembled the 1934 Peugeot Éclipse and the 1957 Ford Fairlane Skyliner. Despite its impressive size, given the limited interior space, the actual shape of the car was extremely subdued. In profile, the front and rear of the vehicle were almost symmetrical.

The Newport, on the other hand, came with a molded grille and the body sides had an indentation ahead of the front wheels, a design element picked up by Buick in 1950. The enveloping coachwork revealed no more than a quarter of the rear wheels.

According to Chrysler's records, some six million American consumers saw the two vehicles while they were on show. Afterwards, however, all twelve were sold as if they were ordinary used cars. American actress Lana Turner purchased the Newport that is now in the Harrah Collection, while movie star Bruce Cabot opted for a Thunderbolt.

138

31.

Ferrari 125S 1947

THE *TIPO* 125 WAS THE fiRST AUTOMOBILE TO BEAR THE NAME "FERRARI." Before World War II, Enzo Ferrari had been impressed by the Packard V12 and the 2.0-litre Delage Grand Prix racers. It was no surprise, then, that he chose to equip his first car with a V12 engine. He hired designer Gioacchino Colombo to build it. Colombo had previously worked on the development of various large displacement engines, including V12s for the Alfa-Romeo 12C and V16s for the 316.

Ferrari 125S 1947

ENGINE
Type: V12, DOHC, three Weber carburetors
Displacement: 1,496 cc. Bore and stroke: 55 mm x 52.5 mm.
Horsepower: 100 hp at 7,000 rpm[4]
DIMENSIONS
Length: 4,500 mm; width: 1,550 mm; height: 1,500 mm; wheelbase: 2,420 mm; weight: 750 kg[5]
TRANSMISSION
5-speed manual
PERFORMANCE
Maximum speed: 170 km/h
COLLECTION
Ferrari North America Inc., Englewood Cliffs, New Jersey

In December 1946, Ferrari called a press conference at his Maranello works to announce his new car line-up: the 125 *Sport*, the 125 *Competizione* and the 125 *Gran Premio*.[1] Later, in 1947, only two 125S models would be built (the "S" stood for Sports). On March 12, Enzo Ferrari took the wheel of the first new car: although it still had to be fitted with a body, he was eager to try it out. Satisfied with the results, he announced to his technicians that the car would take part in a race on an improvised track in the streets of Piacenza on May 11.

The name 125 came simply from the displacement of one cylinder of the car's V12 aluminum engine, i.e., 125 cc.[2] The two cars built in 1947 had different bodies. Number 1C (from the chassis number) had a very simple one-seater body, called the "cigar" by the mechanics in the Maranello works because of its elongated, tubular form.[3] Its wheels were covered with simple motorcycle fenders, while a tiny deflector served as a windshield. The 125S 2C, on the other hand, was fitted with a more elegant body by Milan's Touring coachbuilders. It was more streamlined, its wheels were covered, and the headlights were integrated in the fenders. At Maranello it was called the "wide wings."

However, neither car possessed all the characteristics that would become Ferrari's trademark. Still to come were the rearing black stallion emblem and the Ferrari name stamped on the engine's cylinder head covers.

The 125S had an independent suspension in front and a rigid axle in the rear with cantilever leaf springs. With its tubular chassis,

1 Ferrari/Yates 1991, p. 155.

2 Ibid., p. 144.

3 Ibid., p. 159.

4 Ferrari/Eaton 1989, p. 22.

5 Ferrari/Rancati 1989, p. 37.

the first 125S weighed 750 kg, which was less than its close rival, the Maserati A6.

The 1.5-litre V12 had an output of 72 hp, which enabled the car to reach 46 km/h in first gear, 64 km/h in second, 103 km/h in third, 142 km/h in fourth and 153 km/h in fifth.[6] As stated by Gino Rancati, one of Enzo Ferrari's many biographers: "The 125 was in no way revolutionary. Simply put, it was relatively powerful and its engine was particularly tough. Enzo Ferrari said it himself: 'I build engines, and then put them on wheels.'"[7]

During qualifications for the 99-km Piacenza race, Italian driver Franco Cortese made the best time driving the 125S 2C, while Nino Farina (son of the great Alberto Farina) damaged the 1C and decided, on an impulse, to pull out of the race, although the car could have been repaired in time. Cortese was therefore the sole representative of the Maranello stable in this first race. His Ferrari was the fastest car there, and Cortese was in first place when mechanical problems forced him to withdraw just three laps before the finish.[8]

By July 1947, the two Ferrari 125Ss would take part in nine other races, including two won for Ferrari by the great Tazio Nuvolari. With new rivals like the Maserati A6, however, competition was heating up, and the performance of the 125S paled in comparison. The Ferrari 159, with its more powerful 2.0-litre V12 engine, would soon take up the challenge. In 1948, the Ferrari 166 was introduced. An improved version of the 125 and the 159, it was clearly a more sophisticated automobile and capable of much greater performance. Produced in a number of versions, the Tipo 166 would provide the Ferrari stable with its first decisive victories.

6   Ferrari/Rancati 1989, p. 37.

7   Ibid., p. 37.

8   Ferrari/Yates 1991, p. 164.

32.

Fiat 1100S 50 1947

GIOVANNI AGNELLI, FIAT'S LEGENDARY LEADER, PASSED AWAY ON DECEMBER 16, 1945. He was succeeded by Vittorio Valleta, the man he had named general manager in 1928. It would not be long before Valleta returned Fiat to the heights of its pre-World War II status.

Following the war, Valleta had the Fiat factories and research facilities rebuilt. At a time when Italian political and economic life remained unstable, he had three objectives: "To regain our former ascendancy, to re-establish the prestige of Italian Technology, and to safeguard the jobs of our skilled labour force."[1]

Any prototypes developed during the war had been destroyed in air raids, so in 1945 Fiat was forced to market touched-up and improved 1940 models. One of these was the 1100, or *Millecento* in Italian. Fiat had introduced this automobile in 1937 to replace the aging Balilla. Initially called the 508C, the car was first listed in the 1940 catalogue as the "1100". The 1,089-cc automobile would retain its "1100" designation for the next 32 years.[2]

After building only a few hundred automobiles in 1945, Fiat produced 21,000 units in 1946, more than 70,000 in 1949, and 120,000 in 1951. At this time Fiat's product line included three models: the top-of-the-line 1500, the 500 economy car named *Topolino*, and the intermediate 1100. The company's amazing recovery showed that Valletta had met his original goals, but now he set his sights on re-establishing Fiat's motor racing preeminence.

Accordingly, Fiat developed the 1100S, which was sold from 1947 to 1951. With the introduction of this model, Fiat hoped to recreate a success story of the past, the 1938 508CMM. A racing version of the 508C, the car's bodywork had been designed by Savio for the 1938 *Mille Miglia* – hence the suffix CMM. The car was described by historian Giovanni Lurani as a "svelte two-seater, extended and streamlined at the rear."[3] Driving one of these cars in the *Mille Miglia*, Italian Piero Taruffi outraced all other 1100-cc class participants from start to finish, and took sixteenth place overall.

Fiat 1100S 50 1947

ENGINE
Type: Straight 4-cylinder, overhead valves, 2 Weber downdraft carburetors. Displacement: 1,089 cc. Bore and stroke: 68 mm x 75 mm. Horsepower: 51 hp at 5,200 rpm[4]

DIMENSIONS
Length: 3,900 mm; width: 1,500 mm; height: 1,350 mm; wheelbase: 2,420 mm; weight: 960 kg

TRANSMISSION
4-speed manual

PERFORMANCE
Maximum speed: 150 km/h[5]

COLLECTION
Centro Storico Fiat, Turin, Italy

---

1 Fiat/Sedgwick 1974, p. 235.

2 Ibid., p. 220.

3 Lurani 1981, p. 91.

4 Olyslager 1967, p. 102;
   Fiat/Sedgwick 1974, p. 330.

5 Fiat/Sedgwick 1974, p. 235.

The 508CMM brings to mind the experimental aerodynamic automobiles, with cut-off rear end, designed by Professor W. I. E. Kamm. It is also reminiscent of Hanstein's and Bäumer's amazing BMW 328, with *superleggera*[6] coachwork by Milanese designer Touring, which won the last prewar *Mille Miglia* in 1940.

In an attempt to duplicate the company's 1938 success, Fiat built 401 units of a new performance car derived from its multipurpose 1100 model. The 1100S had a reinforced chassis for driving on rough roads and a 4-cylinder engine that produced 51 hp, some 20 more than the 1100 sedans. As a result, the 1100S could reach a speed of 150 km/h, while the 508CMM could not exceed 140 km/h.

Aesthetically, the 1000S bore a striking resemblance to the 508CMM. Both the side panel and the single side window were retained. The huge rear section prolonged the automobile's roof, as on Professor Kamm's vehicles. In front, however, the 1100S featured a narrow vertical grille in the centre, with a pair of horizontal grilles set lower down on either side; the 508CMM featured a single, large oval grille. Finally, a pair of parking lights replaced the 508CMM's semaphores. Like the 508CMM, the 1100S was a two-seater, but its chassis had an independent front suspension and semi-elliptic leaf springs in the rear.

6   Fiat/Sedgwick 1974, p. 228;
    BMW/Schrader 1979, pp. 344-346.

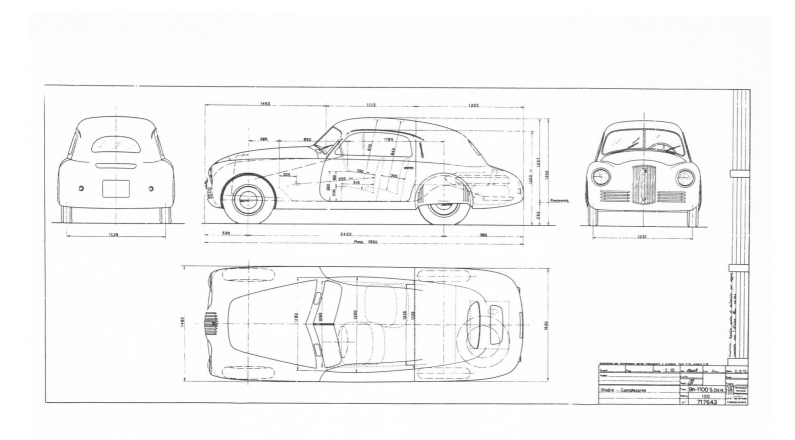

Of the 60 1100-cc class automobiles entered in the first postwar edition of the *Mille Miglia*, in 1947, 50 were Fiats. An 1100S driven by the Brivio/Maggi team finished that race in thirteenth position.

In 1949, a modified 1100S was introduced as the 1100ES. Its 2+2 body by Pinin Farina was mounted on a chassis with a wider rear track. It was on the market until 1952.

33.
Cisitalia-Porsche 360 Grand Prix 1947-1948

PIERO DUSIO, A CAR RACING ENTHUSIAST, DREAMED OF BUILDING HIS OWN Grand Prix automobile. In 1946, using the fortune he had amassed during World War II, he established the Cisitalia company in Turin.

Dusio immediately became involved in motor sports, began producing deluxe sports cars, and launched various other projects.

Some of these projects required the participation of an established car design firm, so the Turin businessman turned his attention to Porsche Büro, which had been located in Gmund, Austria since the end of the war.

He assigned the Gmund team three design projects: an 11-hp tractor, a 1,500-cc sports car, and a Grand Prix single-seater named the 360. Dusio wanted top priority given to the Grand Prix model, and required that a prototype be ready within three months, by September 1947.

The funds advanced by Dusio enabled Ferry Porsche to pay the ransom demanded by the French government for the release of his father, Ferdinand, who had been detained in France since the second half of 1945. In August 1947, the members of Porsche Büro welcomed back Ferdinand Porsche. Dusio's project got under way, despite the immense difficulties involved in producing such a complex vehicle in such a short period of time, especially with Europe in ruins. The results would be astounding.

The 360 came with "on-demand" four-wheel drive and a five-speed transmission, the first to use Porsche's blocking-ring principle. As in the prewar Auto-Union, the engine was mounted behind the driver's compartment. It was a 1.5-litre, flat 12-cylinder, supersquare engine with dual Centric superchargers designed to produce 300 hp. According to some experts, with an efficient tune-up the engine should have been able to produce 385 hp at 10,600 rpm,[1] and attain a speed of 370 km/h. The famous Italian driver, Tazio Nuvolari, volunteered to pilot this rocket.

The 360 had the first modular chassis designed specifically for a Grand Prix car. It was built of tubes of molybdenum-chrome steel. Weight was distributed between front and rear in a 48/52 ratio. Torsion bars provided a four-wheel independent suspension, and

---

Cisitalia-Porsche 360 Grand Prix 1947-1948

ENGINE
Flat 12-cylinder, DOHC, dual Centric superchargers operating in parallel. Displacement: 1,492.6 cc. Bore and stroke: 56 mm x 55 mm. Horsepower: 385 hp at 10,600 rpm[2]

DIMENSIONS
Length: 3,990 mm; width: 1,900 mm; height: 1,200 mm; wheelbase: 2,600 mm; weight: 718.7 kg

TRANSMISSION
5-speed manual

PERFORMANCE
Estimated maximum speed: 300 km/h

COLLECTION
Porsche-Museum, Stuttgart-Zuffenhausen

---

1 Porsche/Seiffert 1989, p. 47.

2 Lawrence 1989, p. 64.

braking depended on four large drums. A simple but aerodynamically efficient body crowned the effort.

Dusio hoped to build six of the cars, along with a sufficient stock of parts to complete a full Grand Prix season. The Turin factory, headed by engineers Carlo Abarth and Rudolf Hruschka, was in fact building up this inventory as work continued. At this point, however, Dusio ran out of money and the 360 could not be completed.

Dusio then announced that he was negotiating with Argentina's dictator Juan Perón to establish a national automobile company in that country. The businessman's creditors were not pleased with this prospect, and Dusio was soon required to repay his debts. Shortly afterward, he left Italy for Argentina.

The 360 would never run on European soil. Tests in South America ended in failure, as the car never exceeded 235.9 km/h.[3] The vehicle was shelved in 1953 and repurchased by Porsche six years later.

3   Lawrence 1989 p. 64.

34.

Porsche 356 "No. 1" 1948

IN 1931, FERDINAND PORSCHE OPENED HIS DESIGN OFFICE IN STUTTGART under the corporate name of Porsche Konstruktionen GmbH. After working for Wanderer, Zündapp, NSU, Auto-Union and Daimler, he secured a mandate to develop the famous Volkswagen. With the outbreak of war, however, he turned his talents to military production.

In November 1944, as the war was entering its final phase, the Porsche team moved to Gmünd, Austria. In July 1945, Porsche was arrested by the French and imprisoned for several months. It was during this period that the Gmünd team came up with the idea of a two-seater convertible sports car derived from the Volkswagen. It was already referred to as the "Porsche."

Upon his release from prison, Ferdinand Porsche was extremely enthusiastic about the idea. Project 356, as it was called, was intended to produce a maximum of 500 automobiles for a clearly defined clientele of wealthy buyers. Before moving ahead with the project, Ferry Porsche conducted market research to assess its feasibility. He also found two Swiss businessmen willing to invest in the Porsche.

On June 11, 1947[1], the "two-seater Volkswagen sport" project was launched. In the Porsche office records, the initial sketches and blueprints bore the number 356, hence the "typ 356" designation of the early production Porsches.

The Porsche "No. 1" featured a tubular chassis. Its engine was situated in front of the rear wheels, while the transmission was behind. The 1.1-litre, air-cooled engine closely resembled the Volkswagen's, and the transmission, suspension and steering were also borrowed from the early Beetle.

In March 1948, the first road trials were held. Thanks to its light alloy body (designed by coachbuilder Friedrich Weber, who had just joined the Porsche team), the new Porsche was capable of attaining a speed of 135 km/h.

The rounded, clean and subdued lines of this convertible were reminiscent of those of Project 64, the prewar aerodynamic coupe. In 1939, three 64s based on the nascent Volkswagen model had

Porsche 356 "No. 1" 1948

ENGINE
Type: flat 4-cylinder, air-cooled. Displacement: 1,131 cc.
Bore and stroke: 64 mm x 75 mm Horsepower: 35 hp at 4,000 rpm

DIMENSIONS
Length: 3,860 mm; width: 1,670 mm; height: 1,250 mm;
wheelbase: 2,150 mm; weight: 596 kg[2]

TRANSMISSION
4-speed manual

PERFORMANCE
Maximum speed: 135 km/h

COLLECTION
Porsche-Museum, Stuttgart-Zuffenhausen

1   Porsche/Conradt 1991, p. 17.

2   Porsche/Boschen and Barth 1978, pp. 28-29.

been produced. (They were scheduled to take part in the Berlin-Rome race, but this was cancelled due to the outbreak of war).

The rear section of the automobile was quite large because of the central placement of the engine. This Porsche was nonetheless the precursor to the production models. Yet even as the trials were taking place, the research department was working on a coupe version. It was also already evident that the tubular chassis would be too expensive. Consequently, a pressed-steel platform chassis would be used for the second generation of Porsches. The engine would be repositioned further back, as in the Volkswagen Beetle; this would provide more space for baggage or passengers. The Porsche we know today was about to be born.

Ferry Porsche at the wheel of the first 356, during a vintage car meet in August 1981.

35.

Tucker 1948

IN THE YEARS FOLLOWING WORLD WAR II, ALL OF AMERICA DREAMED OF better days. The return of the veterans unleashed a frenzy of consumerism that inevitably affected the American auto industry. But none of the big Detroit manufacturers could spark a passion to match that roused in Americans by an obscure car builder named Preston Tucker.

In December 1945, Tucker announced his intention to build "the car of the future." In the spring of 1946, the Tucker Corporation was established. It obtained from the American government the enormous Chicago factory that had been used during the war to construct the Superfortress bomber.

At the same time, Tucker began a widespread advertising campaign to catch the public imagination. Advertisements showed an automobile with ultramodern lines and promised delivery for 1948. "Years ahead of its time!" proclaimed the ads. The Tucker sedan was to be powered by a 9.8-litre transversal rear engine with six opposed cylinders, alloy cylinder heads and variable-timing hydraulic valves.[1] It would turn at 100 rpm when idling, 1,600 rpm at moderate speed, and only 500 rpm at 80 km/h!

With the 1950s around the corner, visionaries throughout the auto industry saw the rear-engine design as the wave of the future, but only Preston Tucker would put this vision into practice.

Tucker hired designer Alex Tremulis, who had begun his career with the Auburn-Cord-Duesenberg group. He created an impressive, fluid body – its drag coefficient (Cd) was estimated at 0.30[2] – marked by a third, central headlight. This Cyclopean eye pivoted to follow the direction of the front wheels.

The curving bodywork hugged the ground – shades of Buck Rogers. The interior was large enough to accommodate six uniformed football players, helmets and all! Moreover, the front and rear bench seats were interchangeable, so that wear could be evenly distributed.

Tucker 1948

ENGINE
Type: rear-mounted, transversal flat 6-cylinder, water-cooled, 2 carburetors. Displacement: 5,477 cc. Bore and stroke: 114 mm x 89 mm. Power: 166 hp at 3,200 rpm

DIMENSIONS
Length: 5,334 mm; width: 2,083 mm; height: 1,651 mm; wheelbase: 3,302 mm; weight: 1,921 kg

TRANSMISSION
4-speed manual with Bendix preselector (vacuum-electric)

PERFORMANCE
Maximum speed: 200 km/h

COLLECTION
The William F. Harrah Foundation National Automobile Museum, Reno, Nevada

1 Ward ed. 1974, p. 2,386.

2 *Fifty Years of American Automobiles, 1939-1989* 1989, p. 376.

Tucker considered passive restraint to be very important, and the sedan was equipped with seat belts, a windshield designed to eject in a collision, and a padded dashboard. The design of the dashboard also included a "safety cave" under the right side, where the occupants of the front seat could take refuge in the instants before a crash.

The project was an enticing one, and Tucker managed to convince businessmen to invest nearly $8 million in his company. However, the development of the engine led to serious delays and increased costs. To obtain the new injection of capital he required, and to satisfy customers who had already paid a deposit on this revolutionary vehicle, Preston Tucker had the company listed on the stock exchange.

Tucker soon decided to shelve the new engine project, opting instead for a Franklin helicopter engine with six opposed cylinders, which would be water-cooled instead of air-cooled. This in turn added significant weight to the vehicle's rear and led to a tendency to oversteer.

When the Tucker was unveiled to the public in 1948, it was different from the automobile promised by its promoter in several other respects. The preproduction models had drum brakes, rather than the disk brakes shown in the prospectus; the motor sported a Stromberg carburetor rather than fuel injection; and the Tuckermatic automatic transmission had been replaced by a Cord 810 manual transmission with preselection. Salvaged from a scrap dealer, these replacements were last-minute additions.

Again looking for new capital to finance further automobile development, Tucker made a loan request to the Securities and Exchange Commission. Not only did the SEC turn him down, but Tucker found himself facing 31 charges, mostly involving fraud. After an expensive four-month trial[3], Tucker was found innocent of the 31 charges[4] against him, but by the time this judgement was handed down in 1950, he had lost all credibility. No more than 51 Tuckers were ever built.

It will never be known whether he was framed or indeed a crook. Whatever the case, Preston Tucker ranks among the first to revitalize the American dream in the postwar era.

3 Tucker/Woron 1988, p. 196.

4 *Fifty Years of American Automobiles, 1939-1989* 1989, p. 376.

36.

Bentley Mark VI Pinin Farina 1949

THE FIRST EXAMPLES OF THE BENTLEY MARK VI WERE PRODUCED IN 1946, just after the war. The chassis, with independent front suspension and coil springs, was the same one used on the prewar Mark V. (Earlier Bentleys used a front suspension with semi-elliptic leaf springs.)

The Mark VI was also the first Bentley to have a welded steel body. As such, it became the first mass-produced car built by a manufacturer that had previously offered only custom-made vehicles This new commercial approach signified the end of the hand-built Bentley.

The change resulted from an increased integration of Bentley operations within Rolls-Royce. This was intended to maximize the sharing of Rolls-Royce components. It came as no surprise, then, when the Rolls-Royce Silver Dawn, unveiled in July 1949, used the same engine – a 6-cylinder with overhead and side valves – and body as the Mark VI (with the exception of the grille).

This increased standardization did not, however, stop the independent coachbuilders, who continued to offer personalized versions of the Mark VI. Figoni and Falaschi, Facel Métalon, Ramseir and Pinin Farina all created different versions.

For the Geneva Motor Show, Pinin Farina adopted traditional British styling, creating two extremely classic bodies for the Mark VI chassis. One was a coupe, with the profile of a cabriolet. British coachbuilders of the period referred to the style as the drop-head coupe.

Despite their classic appearance, the Pinin Farina models looked very different from those sold by Bentley. The headlights, for example, were not squeezed between the grille and the fenders, as on the stock Mark VI. Rather, they were mounted ahead of the fenders, which gave a lighter look to the front of the car. Pinin Farina's two-piece windshield also gave a more streamlined shape to a car that might otherwise have had a sterner look. Finally, the Turin coachbuilder gave the rear fenders the more elongated, detached appearance that Rolls-Royce itself would adopt for the Bentley Type R Continental model it built from 1952 to 1955.

Bentley Mark VI Pinin Farina 1949

ENGINE
Type: straight 6, two SU carburetors. Displacement: 4,257 cc. Bore and stroke: 89 mm x 114 mm. Horsepower: 135 hp

DIMENSIONS
Length: 5,230 mm; width: 1,830 mm; height: not provided; wheelbase: 3,050 mm; weight: 1,242 kg (chassis)

TRANSMISSION
4-speed manual

PERFORMANCE
Maximum speed: 150 km/h

COLLECTION
Phil J. Chartrand Collection

The Pinin Farina cabriolet was purchased by a Swiss client following the Geneva show. He would keep it until his death. It was brought into Canada in 1974 by a collector who dismantled the entire vehicle with a view to restoring it. However, this task would have to wait until the late 1980s, when it was carried out by another collector, Richard Grenon, who worked for the Montreal firm, Au-Temps-Tic Auto.

ERRATUM

Bentley Mark VI
Pinin Farina 1949

The first sentence of the last paragraph on page 157 should read as follows:

The first owner of this automobile was Dr. Willi Spieler of Zurich. He purchased the chassis from Rolls-Royce in 1948 and had the coachwork designed and built by Battista Pinin Farina in Turin. It was delivered to Dr. Spieler at the Geneva International Automobile Exhibition in 1949.

37.

Alfa-Romeo 1900 Disco volante 1952

FOR ALFA-ROMEO, THE *DISCO VOLANTE* PROJECT ("FLYING SAUCER" IN Italian) played a developmental role, as well as serving promotional purposes. In 1952, Alfa's test driver, Consalvo Sanesi, first circled the Monza racetrack in the new concept car designed by Milan's Touring coachbuilders.

On the Monza track, the new two-seater revealed an astonishingly sleek silhouette; Touring described the shape as lenticular and biconvex.[1] But the project was not just an exercise in aesthetics. The *Disco volante* was meant to provide less resistance to crosswinds, and it featured faired-in wheels, front as well as rear, that were better integrated with the body.

While the automobile was undeniably elegant, the design of the coachwork was rather impractical on winding roads, because of its limited manoeuvrability. A second, narrower *Disco volante* (the *Disco volante a fianchi stretti*) was built to rectify this problem, and versions produced from 1953 on no longer featured faired-in wheels.

The first *Disco volante* had a spartan interior. The two seats were simple cushions separated by a very prominent transmission tunnel. The transmission tunnel and the insides of the small doors were padded to offset the poor seating and mitigate the effects of centrifugal force while cornering.

The aluminum *superleggera*-type coachwork was very low, making the wheel arches very prominent against the belt line. The top of the body featured two long ribs behind the passenger compartment and a deep recess in the rear to hold the standard Italian licence plate.

Engineer Rudolf Hruska was responsible for reorganizing production of the Alfa-Romeo 1900 between 1951 and 1954. He sensed that the promotional possibilities of the *Disco volante* could be used to revive Alfa's fortunes and draw attention to the 1900 models. (The first *Disco volante* had been built using a modified version of the 1900's mechanical components.) A few *Disco volantes* were therefore prepared for the racing circuit. The great Juan Manuel Fangio drove one to a second place finish at the

---

Alfa-Romeo 1900 *Disco-volante* 1952

ENGINE
Type: in-line 4-cylinder. Displacement: 1,997 cc. Bore: 85 mm; stroke: not provided. Horsepower: 158 hp

DIMENSIONS
Length: 4,000 mm; width: 1,900 mm; height: 4,040 mm; wheelbase: 2,220 mm; weight: 735 kg

TRANSMISSION
4-speed manual

PERFORMANCE
Maximum speed: 225 km/h

COLLECTION
Museo Storico Alfa-Romeo, Arese, Italy

---

1   Touring/Anderloni and Anselmi 1983, p. 202

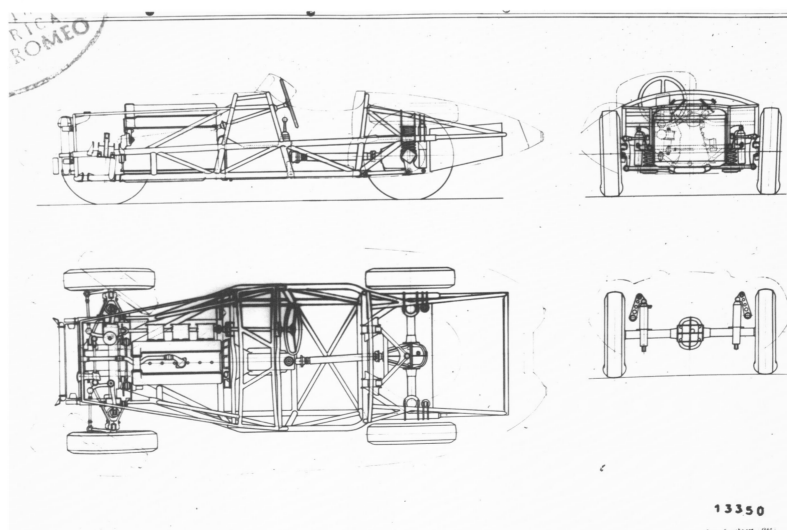

A view of the chassis and the suspension of the Alfa-Romeo 1900 *Disco volante*

1953 *Mille Miglia*, despite defective steering! But the *Disco volante*'s racing career was to be short-lived since it could not rival the power of its competitors.[2]

The silhouette of the *Disco volante* nonetheless inspired Jaguar's design for the 1956-57 D-type Jaguar and, even more noticeably, for the E-type, which went on the market in 1961.

The *Disco volante* was designed by one of the great Italian coachbuilders of the era, Carrozzeria Touring, founded by Felice Bianchi Anderloni in 1926. Touring subsequently designed numerous bodies for BMW, Alfa-Romeo, Aston Martin and even Hudson, among others. Touring also designed the body for the precursor of the Ferraris, the "815." The company closed its doors in 1966.

2   Tragatsch 1971, p. 46.

38.

Mercedes-Benz W196 Stromlinienwagen 1954

ENCOURAGED BY THE PERFORMANCE OF ITS 300 SL AND SLR MODELS IN Sports Car Championship racing, Mercedes returned to Grand Prix competition in 1954. Under the leadership of professor Fritz Nallinger[1], the Stuttgart manufacturer perfected an automobile that was revolutionary mainly because of its streamlined bodywork (at the time, Grand Prix automobiles were still open-wheeled).

The new single-seater was named the W196 *Stromlinienwagen* [streamlined car]. The mechanics, which were carried over from the 300 SL gull-wing coupe, included a straight 8-cylinder engine with desmodromic valves. The valves were operated by a return mechanism instead of springs. The purpose of this feature was to enable the engine to run hard for extended periods. The engine consisted of two blocks of four cylinders, with the timing gear and power take-off set between them in the middle of the crankshaft. Displacement was 2,496 cc and power output 257 hp. In 1955, output was increased to 290 hp. The automobile also featured oversized drum brakes all around, and independent front and rear suspension.

The W196 first competed in the Reims Grand Prix in July 1954. On the big triangular circuit, which consisted of straightaways that allowed the cars to reach maximum speeds, the W196 *Stromlinienwagen* took the first three positions, thanks to talented driving by team pilots Fangio, Kling and Hermann. However, things were different in the next event, the English Grand Prix. The Mercedes drivers, who literally could not see their wheels, had trouble positioning their automobiles to take the curves of the winding Silverstone racetrack. Fangio barely managed to finish in fourth position.

From then on, the competition unit at Mercedes devised open-wheeled W196s for winding tracks. In 1955, Mercedes would even build chassis on a variety of wheelbases for use on specific racetracks.

This strategy was to pay dividends as Juan Manuel Fangio took the German Grand Prix on the Nürburgring track, and the Swiss Grand Prix in Berne, both held on winding circuits.

Mercedes-Benz W196 *Stromlinienwagen* 1954

ENGINE
Type: straight 8. Displacement: 2,496 cc. Bore and stroke: 76 mm x 68.8 mm. Horsepower: 257 hp at 8,200 rpm[2]

DIMENSIONS
Length: 4,200 mm; width: 1,680 mm; height: 1,020 mm; wheelbase: not provided; weight: 700 kg

TRANSMISSION
5-speed manual

PERFORMANCE
Maximum speed: 275 km/h

COLLECTION
Mercedes-Benz-Museum, Stuttgart

---

1   Mercedes-Benz/Cimarosti 1986, p. 83.

2   Lawrence 1989, p. 217.

The streamlined body was nonetheless a masterpiece of aerodynamic design. Devoid of sharp angles, the clean flowing lines of this very low-set automobile had been wind-tunnel tested. To reduce height to a minimum, the engine was set in a near-horizontal position (mounted at 37° on the automobile's space frame[3]). Even the drive shaft was repositioned to lower the driver's seat. The particularly wide track of the W196 let drivers take advantage of a very low centre of gravity, which produced excellent roadholding on fast circuits.

Juan Manuel Fangio took the World Driving Championship at the end of the 1954 racing season and again in 1955, the same year that Mercedes won the Constructors Championship. In fifteen starts over two years of Grand Prix competition, streamlined and open-wheeled W196s chalked up twelve wins. These included seven top-two finishes, as well as a top-three and a top-four placing. Following this

3   Nye 1993, p. 69.

sweep, Mercedes decided to discontinue its participation in Grand Prix racing and to focus on the Sports Car Championship. It would eventually return to the Grand Prix circuit in 1992 with the Sauber racing stable.

The starting line for the 1954 French Grand Prix in Reims. Car number 18 is driven by Juan Manuel Fangio, number 20 by Karl Kling and number 22 by Hans Herrmann.

Photo: Mercedes-Benz Archiv

Fangio and Kling during the 1954
French Grand Prix in Reims.

Photo: Mercedes-Benz Fotodienst

The 1954 Italian Grand Prix in Monza.

39.

Jaguar D 1955

JAGUAR'S FOUNDER, SIR WILLIAM LYONS, WAS CONVINCED THAT ENDURANCE events, such as the Le Mans 24-hour race, were the best showcases for a car's features. In 1951, P. N. Whitehead had won the famous event in a XK-120C, C-type Jaguar (C for competition). In 1953, the Rolt-Hamilton team also used a C to accomplish the same feat, but the model, closely related to the XK-120 production automobile, was starting to show its limits.

To replace it, the company developed the D-type Jaguar. Shorter and lighter, the D was launched in May 1954. It had a low-slung appearance and the bodywork, designed by aerodynamics engineer Malcolm Sayer[1], had pronounced curves. It also featured a characteristic rear fin on the right side. This appendage acted like a rudder to enhance the car's longitudinal stability, necessary in an automobile that could reach 100 km/h in under five seconds thanks to its 6-cylinder, 250-hp engine. From 1955 to 1957, the D would log three consecutive wins at Le Mans.

The body design was the result of wind-tunnel research; even the rear-view mirrors were tested for wind resistance. The D's drag coefficient was 28% lower than that of the C, and by lowering the car even more in 1955, a further 36% decrease was achieved. The D's superior aerodynamic efficiency was also evident in its lower fuel consumption compared to the C.

The shape of the new single-seater was one factor that lead to the adoption of disk brakes on all four wheels. The car's bulk, which "naturally" slowed it down, was reduced, and this meant that a more efficient braking system was required. Disk brakes developed by Dunlop for the 1953 C were chosen. Ferrari followed suit in 1959, using disk brakes on its Testa Rossa 250.

The D's aluminum body covered an innovative structure. Given the magnesium-alloy, monocoque design of the chassis, the body itself became a structural component. The body panels were riveted to an oval beam that ran lengthwise through the centre of the car. Colin Chapman adopted the same structure for his 1962 Lotus 25.

Jaguar D 1955

ENGINE
Type: 6 cylinder in-line, DOHC, 3 Weber carburetors. Displacement: 3,442 cc. Bore and stroke: 87 mm x 106 mm. Horsepower: 285 hp at 5,750 rpm

DIMENSIONS
Length: 4,102 mm; width: 1,661 mm; height: 1,143 mm; wheelbase: 2,301 mm; weight: 971 kg

TRANSMISSION
4-speed manual with synchromesh

PERFORMANCE
Maximum speed: 259 km/h

COLLECTION
Rosso Bianco Collection, Aschaffenburg, Germany

1   Casucci 1981, p.157.

Tubular subframes supported the engine, transmission, rear axle and two fuel tanks (these were rubber tanks in metal alloy casings, to increase impact resistance, as found on the 1953 C-type). The effective rack-and-pinion steering would later be used on the production XK-140.

The 3.4-litre, 6-cylinder engine came from the Mark VII sedan. It had alloy cylinder heads with hemispheric combustion chambers and a dry-sump lubrication system. This made it possible to set the engine deeper in the chassis and thus lower the centre of gravity.

In 1955, many alterations were made to the D's body. The front overhang was increased and the Perspex windshield was raised and extended to the tail-fin, which was also extended. The head-rest was faired in. Engine displacement was increased from 3.4 to 3.8 litres and power output was raised to 270 hp.

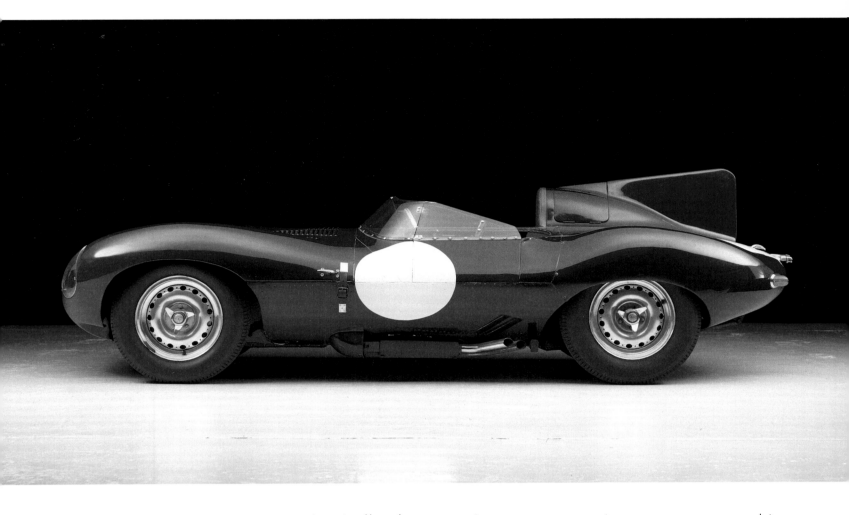

Ironically, the event Lyons was counting on to promote his automobiles was marred by disaster. During the 1955 Le Mans race, a Mercedes-Benz driven by Pierre Levegh crashed and catapulted into the crowd, killing 83 spectators and injuring over a hundred others. Jaguar won the race but, given the tragic turn of events, it was hardly a triumph.

A type D driven by Flockhart and Sanderson won the 1956 Le Mans race under happier circumstances and, in 1957, Flockhart and Bueb's D competed and won for the Scottish stable. In October 1956, Jaguar had announced it would be withdrawing from competition. In the world of racing, automobiles quickly become obsolete, and the British manufacturer did not wish to invest further in a replacement for the D.

40.

Cadillac 57-70 Eldorado Brougham 1957

AT THE END OF THE 1950s, COMPETITION AMONG DETROIT'S BIG THREE auto manufacturers – GM, Ford and Chrysler – had an impact on all levels of the automotive industry, including the luxury automobile market. When, in 1956, Ford introduced its Continental Mark II at almost $10,000 US, Chrysler responded with a new prestige automobile, the Imperial four-door sedan, with body by the Italian firm, Ghia. In March 1957,[1] Cadillac unveiled its own hand-built luxury sedan, the Eldorado Brougham, manufactured in the United States by the Fleetwood coachbuilders.

The Eldorado Brougham was the result of a development process that had produced the Cadillac Park Avenue and Cadillac Orleans show cars, unveiled by General Motors in 1953 and 1954, respectively. Designed by stylist Ed Glowacke, the Eldorado was the first American hardtop. Its design eliminated the central pillar that conventionally supported a sedan's roof. The model was also equipped with "suicide" rear doors.

The price of the Eldorado Brougham was well above that of the Ford Continental Mark II. This made it the most expensive car in America.

While the styling of the Continental could be described as relatively unadorned and subdued, the Eldorado Brougham was a more exuberant car. Striking colour, chrome trim and a stainless steel roof all enhanced its luxurious appearance. Double headlights were featured on either side of the grille. (This was a first in American automotive history, an honour that was shared with the 1957 Nash.) The Cadillac was truly a "dream car".

The 1950s Cadillac was also known for its vertical tail fins, a feature that had made its first, rather timid appearance on the 1948 model. Harley Earl,[2] head of design at GM, drew his inspiration from the tail fins of the Lockheed P-38 Lightning, a World War II fighter plane. Fins were soon added to most American models and to a few European automobiles as well.

To ensure the highest standard of comfort for the passengers of its prestige automobile, Cadillac engineers had developed an air

Cadillac 57-70 Eldorado Brougham 1957

ENGINE
Type: 90° V-8 with overhead valves, two 4-barrel Carter carburetors.
Displacement: 5,983 cc. Bore and stroke: 101.6 mm x 92 mm.
Horsepower: 325 hp at 4,800 rpm

DIMENSIONS
Length: 5,494 mm; width: 2,050 mm; height: 1,501 mm; wheelbase: 3,200 mm; weight: 2,413 kg

TRANSMISSION
Automatic

PERFORMANCE
Maximum speed: not provided

COLLECTION
Private collection

1 Gunnell 1982, p. 104.

2 Nesbitt 1985, p. 27.

suspension system. (Citroën had introduced a hydropneumatic suspension in 1955.) However, the Eldorado's air suspension tended to break down. GM quickly replaced many of these systems with less comfortable but much more reliable coil springs.

A symbol of opulence evocative of a period of prosperity, Cadillac offered a wide range of optional equipment and accessories. You could purchase six magnetic, silver-plated tumblers for the glove compartment, or an Arpège atomizer containing Lanvin's Arpège perfume, not to mention the 44 fabric and colour combinations available for the interior upholstery.

The Eldorado Brougham also featured many technical innovations as standard equipment, including low-profile tires, a remote-control trunk lid opener, a power seat with a memory feature, and even air conditioning.

Only a handful of these vehicles were made: 400 in 1957[3] and no more than 300 the following year.[4] In 1959 and 1960, Cadillac followed Chrysler's lead and had the coachwork of its prestige models prepared in Italy by Pininfarina.

Ironically, by 1958 the Continental Mk II had already been replaced by the less expensive Continental Mk III. The earlier car, marketed as a limited-edition model in 1956 and 1957, had been Ford's competition against the Eldorado Brougham. The Mk III would be much more successful than either the American Broughams or the subsequent Italian versions.

3   Cadillac/Hendry 1990, p. 458.

4   Langworth 1992, p. 91.

41.

Porsche 936/77 Spyder 1977

IN 1976, THE FÉDÉRATION INTERNATIONALE DE L'AUTOMOBILE Z SET UP two new classes for competition automobiles. Group 5, or "Silhouette" class, consisted of automobiles derived from production models and entered in competition at the Constructor's World Championship. Group 6, or "Prototype" class, consisted of cars competing in the Sports Car World Championship. Although the FIA had decreed that automobiles of the two classes should never run in the same event, the Automobile Club de l'Ouest, organizer of the Le Mans 24-hour race, decided otherwise.

It was obvious to Porsche's management that Group 6 cars would have an advantage at Le Mans. Consequently, although the company had to this point budgeted most of its development money for its 935 Silhouette model, Porsche decided to invest in the development of a 936 Group 6 Prototype. The project was given the green light in September 1975. As early as the following February, the first prototype, until then a well-kept secret, began circling the Paul Ricard circuit in France.

The 936 borrowed many components from previous models. The chassis was based on that of the former 908, while the 5-speed transmission and braking system came from the 917. The new car's body was also very reminiscent of the 917. With its wide, open body, huge rear aerodynamic deflectors, and prominent air intakes to supply and cool the engine, the 936 would become the quintessential single-seater prototype of the late 1970s.

Meanwhile, Porsche's main competitor, Renault-Alpine, had produced two automobiles with turbocharged V6 engines. In February, however, Renault-Alpine management was not aware of the danger hanging over its automobiles.

During their first confrontation, the Porsche 936 and the Renault-Alpine both experienced an array of technical problems. But after this encounter, the Porsche Spyders would always defeat the French automobile.

Porsche 936/77 Spyder 1977

ENGINE
Type: flat 6-cylinder, 2 KKK turbochargers. Displacement: 2,142 cc. Bore and stroke: 83 mm x 66 mm. Horsepower: 540 hp at 8,000 rpm

DIMENSIONS
Length: 4,250 mm; width: 1,981 mm; height: 960 mm; wheelbase: 2,400 mm; weight: 700 kg

TRANSMISSION
5-speed manual

PERFORMANCE
Maximum speed: 350 km/h

COLLECTION
Porsche-Museum, Stuttgart-Zuffenhausen, Germany

The 936 won its first major victory at Le Mans, with Belgian pilot Jacky Ickx taking first place. This marked the third win at Le Mans for both Porsche and Ickx.

For the 1977 racing season, Porsche and Renault both decided to confine their Le Mans effort to Group 6 automobiles, because of their great media value. On other circuits, Porsche remained heavily involved in Group 5 championship competition.

The Spyder 936/77, whose bodywork now displayed the bright Martini colors, featured a 540-hp engine equipped with two KKK turbochargers. The front track was reduced slightly, and the front section of the body was modified to increase speed. As a result, the 936/77 was able to gain an additional 24 km/h on the Mulsanne straight at Le Mans.

Renault entered three automobiles in the 1977 Le Mans, while Porsche decided to run only two. Soon after the start of the event, Ickx's Porsche had to be withdrawn due to mechanical failure. The

Belgian driver, running 29 minutes behind, returned to the race in the second car. Gradually, Ickx managed to overtake the front-running Renaults and win the event in dramatic fashion.

The 936 returned to Le Mans in 1978 and 1979 but did not enjoy the same success. In 1980, Porsche focussed its efforts at Le Mans on the 924 Carrera GT, but was, once again, unsuccessful. Then, in 1981, completely overhauled 936s made an unexpected comeback, providing a fifth Le Mans victory both for Porsche and for Belgian pilot Jacky Ickx. Ickx's fifth triumph was unprecedented in the history of the 24-hour event.

42

Mercedes-Benz C-111/III 1978

THE C-111/III WAS BUILT BY MERCEDES-BENZ TO TEST ITS DIESEL ENGINE AND also to gain a better understanding of the effect of air flow on an automobile body. The 5-cylinder engine, with a Garrett turbocharger, was developed from the engine in the 300SD production sedan, but was twice as powerful. The C-111/III's increased power, reduced weight and excellent streamlining enabled it to beat nine world records, some of which had stood for 38 years.

The four drivers were the French journalist Paul Frère, who was also a renowned auto expert and former race car driver, the Swiss Rico Steinemann, a former journalist and race car driver who was public relations director for Mercedes-Benz Switzerland, and Hans Liebold and Guido Moch, two engineers from the Stuttgart firm.

On the Nardo test track the four drivers took turns piloting the Mercedes for 2 1/2-hour shifts, for a total of 12 hours non-stop. These were long hours, with fog reducing visibility to 75 metres. Difficult conditions for driving at 300 km/h!

The car's polyester bodywork, reinforced with carbon fibre and fibreglass, was completely streamlined. Its drag coefficient was only 0.195, and made it quite clear that efficiency was the car's raison d'être.

The vehicle broke the following records during that April of 1978: 316.484 km/h over 100 kilometres; 319.835 km/h over 100 miles; 321.860 km/h over 500 kilometres; 320.788 km/h over 500 miles; 318.308 km/h over 1,000 kilometres; 319.091 km/h over 1,000 miles; 321.843 km/h over one hour; 317.796 km/h over six hours; and finally, 314.463 km/h over 12 hours.

This C-111/111 was part of a family of experimental vehicles begun in 1969. Clad in orange and black, the first C-111 served to test various technologies: a centrally mounted Wankel rotary engine, a new type of suspension, and the use of plastic body materials. In June 1976, the C-111/IID, also equipped with a turbo-diesel engine, established three world records and 16 more in its class on the Nardo track.

The C-111/III served to show the remarkable abilities of the diesel engine in the areas of fuel consumption and durability. The

Mercedes-Benz C-111/III 1978

Engine

Type: in-line 5-cylinder diesel with Garrett turbocharger.
Displacement: 3,005 cc. Bore and stroke: 91 mm x 92.4 mm.
Horsepower: 230 hp at 4,400-4,600 rpm

Dimensions

Length: 5,480 mm; width: 1,750 mm; height: 1,100 mm;
wheelbase: 2,720 mm; weight: 1,245 kg

TRANSMISSION
5-speed manual

PERFORMANCE
Maximum speed: 325 km/h[1]

COLLECTION
Mercedes-Benz-Museum, Stuttgart

1 Press release, MSG 58.

The Mercedes-Benz C-111/III on the Nardo circuit in April 1978.

Photo: Daimler-Benz-Archiv-Foto

car also showed the engine's performance potential at a time when fuel consumption had become a particularly important consideration. This was the reason given for the prototype's appearance at international auto shows, including the Montreal show in 1980. The main argument was simple: despite the high speeds achieved by the C-111/III during the trials, it had maintained an average fuel consumption of only 16 l/100 km, or slightly less than a 1978 Ford Thunderbird.

The presentation of the C-111/III at auto shows also served as a reminder that Mercedes-Benz had been selling automobiles equipped with diesel engines since 1936. During the period when the C-111/III was achieving its world records, half of Mercedes-Benz's annual production consisted of diesel-powered cars.

43.

Chaparral-Cosworth 2K 1979

THE HISTORY OF THE CHAPARRAL 2K BEGINS IN 1979. ENTERED IN THE American Indy CART championship, which included the Indianapolis 500, the car was held back by numerous mechanical failures. Nonetheless, the Chaparral's driver, Al Unser, managed to pull off a victory in the last race of the season in Phoenix, Arizona.

Although the car did not win the Indy 500 in 1979, it was awarded the Louis Schwitzer prize, which is presented to the most original one-seater entered in the Indy.

It was Jim Hall who came up with the original idea behind the Chaparral. To put the concept into practice, he turned to British engineer John Barnard (who in 1994 was one of Ferrari's engineers). The result was a ground-effect automobile with an aluminum monocoque chassis that was produced in England by BS Fabrications.

The Chaparral's dimensions were comparable to those of a Ferrari 312T4, which Jody Scheckter used to win the 1979 Formula 1 championship. Another common characteristic with Formula 1 one-seaters was the use of a Ford-Cosworth V8 engine. The version of this turbocharged DFX engine used in the Chaparral was methanol-fuelled and provided 700 hp.

The Chaparral-Cosworth 2K marked a turning point in automobile design. Designed for racing, the car made maximum use of aerodynamics with its fins, deflectors and wind-tunnel-tested shape. The driver was an integral part of this shape, and it was necessary to adjust the spoiler according to the size of the pilot. Use of the ground effect also implied a careful design of the car's undercarriage.

In 1980, Jim Hall hired driver Johnny Rutherford to pilot the bright yellow racer. Only one car would go through the entire racing season, but the goal remained an Indy 500 victory.

The Chaparral still had to face competition from the powerful Penske stable, which included three PC9 single-seaters piloted by highly talented drivers: Mario Andretti, Bobby Unser and Rick Mears.

> **Chaparral-Cosworth 2K 1979**
> **ENGINE**
> Type: turbocharged Ford-Cosworth V8. Displacement: 1,650 cc. Bore and stroke: not provided. Horsepower: 700 hp at 9,500 rpm[1]
> **DIMENSIONS**
> Length: 4,572 mm; width: 2,010 mm; height: not provided; wheelbase: 2,692 mm; weight: not provided
> **TRANSMISSION**
> 4-speed manual
> **PERFORMANCE**
> Maximum speed: 309.406 km/h
> **COLLECTION**
> Indianapolis Motor Speedway Hall of Fame Museum, Indianapolis

1 Chaparral/Lamm 1980, p. 53.

Ironically, various mechanical problems would ensure that none of the Penske PC9s would actually complete the Indy 500. Johnny Rutherford took the 64th edition of the Indianapolis 500 before 300,000 spectators. The victory would be one of five achieved during the season's 12 races (with one exception, Penske cars took all the other races).

Rutherford would win one more victory, the last for the Chaparral, in the opening race of the Indy CART season in Phoenix in 1981.

44.

Ferrari F1/87 1987

IN 1987, THE FERRARI STABLE TOOK A NEW DIRECTION. EVER SINCE ITS victory at the German Grand Prix in August 1985, the *scuderia* had not placed a single driver at the summit of the winners' podium. Now, with the fortieth Grand Prix season coming up, everyone at Ferrari was eager to get back on the road to success.

The season kicked off with a new one-seater, the F1/87. It was largely the result of work by a committee made up of Gustav Brunner, then chief designer at Ferrari (he had formerly been a designer with the ATS stable), Harvey Postlethwaite, an engineer and chassis specialist and two former members of the Renault stable, the aerodynamicist Jean-Claude Migeot and the driver Jean-Jacques His.

In November 1986, the famous British engineer John Barnard, who until then had been with McLaren, joined the stable as director of engineering. He categorically refused, however, to move to Italy, preferring instead to work at the Guilford Technical Office or GTO, a series of installations set up at Shalford in England.

The mandate of the GTO was to ensure the development and perfection of new one-seater Ferraris. This "transplantation" outside the motherland of Ferrari's hallowed Formula 1 design department did not sit well with everyone at Maranello. It was, however, the price to be paid for the great talent of their new engineer.

When Barnard joined Ferrari, the development of the new one-seater was well under way. The shape of the chassis and front of the car, as well as the type of suspension, had already been established. Barnard's influence within Ferrari would become more evident in 1988 and 1989 when the new F1, with an aspirated engine meant to replace the former F1's turbocharged engine, was put on the road. Thus the F1/87 was to some extent a temporary model.

The F1/87 came equipped with a new 90° V6 engine dubbed the 033. Il was combined with a new in-line 6-speed manual gearbox. Driver Michele Alboreto would take the controls of the F1/87 numbered 27. In 1984, he was the first Italian Formula 1 driver to be hired by Ferrari since 1975. His new team mate would be the Austrian Gerhard Berger, who would drive car number 28.

Ferrari F1/87 1987

ENGINE
Type: 24-valve, V6. Displacement: 1,496 cc. Bore and stroke: 81 mm x 48.4 mm. Horsepower: 880 hp at 11,500 rpm

DIMENSIONS
Length: 4,229 mm; width: 2,120 mm; height: 1,000 mm; wheelbase: 2,800 mm; weight: 542 kg

TRANSMISSION
6-speed manual

PERFORMANCE
Maximum speed: not provided

COLLECTION
Ferrari North America Inc., Englewood Cliffs, New Jersey

The F1/87 was distinguished by front spoilers equipped with flaps, enormous pontoons with a double air intake, and very high and angular rear fins.

The season was plagued by a variety of malfunctions. Ferrari's engineers had to work hard to keep up with the powerful cars of McLaren-Honda and TAG-Porsche. However, their dogged perseverance paid off early in the season, with two third-place finishes by Alboreto at San Marino and Monaco, a second-place standing picked up by Berger at the Portugal Grand Prix and, finally, with two victories by the same driver during the last races of the season in Japan and Australia.

The 1988 season began with a development of the F1/87 and a good dose of enthusiasm. Then, in August 1988, the Ferrari stable turned a new leaf in its history with the death of its celebrated *commandatore*, Enzo Ferrari, at the age of 90. Fiat then took over the stable.

45.

Ferrari Mythos Pininfarina 1989

PININFARINA UNVEILED THE FERRARI MYTHOS IN OCTOBER 1989, DURING THE Tokyo Auto show. This was the Italian stylist's first official incursion into a major salon outside Europe. The choice of Japan was not fortuitous: since 1980, the Japanese have surpassed the Americans in the production of automobiles[1].

For Pininfarina, the Ferrari Mythos also constituted a return to the eccentric era of dream cars. Its *barchetta*-style carbon fibre body is evocative in this respect: although distinct, the front and rear volumes intersect to generate a provocative shape devoid of anything artificial or non-functional.

The Mythos has neither a roof nor side windows, and its sharply inclined windshield recalls Group C racing cars. Pininfarina wanted to create a two-seater with an undeniably sporty look. The spartan interior reflects the same philosophy, reduced as it is to two formfitting seats and a pared-down instrument panel. A module comprised of the steering wheel, dashboard (with circular analogue dials) and pedals can be adjusted laterally to suit the driver.

One should not, however, see this vehicle as a gratuitous exercise in style. In modern high-performance cars, the centre-rear positioning of the engine is an interesting formula that makes it possible to improve on the distribution of masses and the front body profile without compromising roominess and comfort. For the Mythos, Pininfarina opted for the chassis and the 4.9-litre, flat 12-cylinder engine of the Ferrari Testarossa. While the front of the car remains narrow, the rear radiators bracketing the chassis make a wider track necessary. The designers' decision to have the body composed of two separate volumes intersecting at the passenger compartment was motivated by a desire to compensate for the discrepancy between the front and rear masses.

The Mythos is still more compact that the Ferrari that inspired it. It is 180 mm shorter, mainly because of the considerably reduced rear overhang. However, its width has increased by 135 mm due to the wider rear track.

The highly uniform profile is dominated by overlapping planes, a feature that resulted from the rear placement of the radiators. The

Ferrari Mythos Pininfarina 1989
ENGINE
Type: 48-valve, flat 12-cylinder. Displacement: 4,942 cc. Bore and stroke: 82 mm x 78 mm. Horsepower: 390 hp at 6,300 rpm
DIMENSIONS
Length: 4,305 mm; width: 2,100 mm; height: 1,065 mm; wheelbase: 2,550 mm; weight: 1,250 kg
TRANSMISSION
5-speed manual
PERFORMANCE
Maximum speed: not provided
COLLECTION
Pininfarina

1   Motor Vehicle Manufacturers Assn. *1992*, pp. 8-13.

190

side air intake, which has a more inclined aperture than that of the Testarossa, displays a certain formal purity: the Testarossa's five fins have disappeared. The designers strove to integrate the essential components within an overall form, thereby making their presence more discreet. The extremely low front body was provided with fixed headlights, instead of the retractable headlights of the assembly-line model. A pared-down rear design made it possible to integrate design and functional elements (brake lights, bumpers, exhaust, etc.) to the point where one can no longer distinguish the large mobile fin.

When the car attains a speed of 100 km/h, this fin automatically rises a distance of 300 mm and pivots 12°. At the same time, a small retractable flap advances by 30 mm. At high speeds, the combined effect of these two aerodynamic correctors reduces the Mythos's lift by 50%; thus, at 250 km/h, the raised and rotated rear fin should exert a pressure of 150 kg on the car. To simplify parking manoeuvres, these two deflectors return to their initial position when the speed of the car drops below 70 km/h. With this automobile, Pininfarina shows how a style, and a bold style at that, can possess truly functional and effective features.

46.
Pininfarina Ethos 1992

IN A SOCIETY THAT PROTECTS THE ENVIRONMENT BY IMPOSING REGULATIONS, the four vehicles produced by Pininfarina's Ethos project show that it is possible to produce vehicles compatible with the world of tomorrow.

Ethos is a Greek word meaning "standard of life, custom and ethics." For the first exponent of its Ethos project, Pininfarina chose to produce an automobile with plenty of personality. The open body style seems totally appropriate. The curved lines seem sculpted by the wind, intended to place the car firmly in the tradition of the Italian sports car.

The design was the work of a young Swiss stylist, Stefan Schwarz. The result was a compact car, similar in size to the new Fiat Coupé. The "barquette" (from the Italian *barchetta*, or small craft) is a two-seater with an aggressive but very aerodynamically efficient shape – its drag coefficient is 0.34. The machine is powered by a centrally mounted Orbital engine.

The Ethos was also intended to be an example of synchronized development. All of the Pininfarina groups involved in the development of the Ethos I worked together, to ensure that the work progressed in tandem. The aim was to reduce overall development time, but also to solve problems as soon as they appeared. There is no doubt that this approach guaranteed the feasibility of all aspects of the project.

Still, the Ethos was intended above all to meet strict fuel consumption and pollution reduction requirements. The choice of green for the body was undoubtedly deliberate.

The first objective, therefore, was to keep weight to a minimum. The goal of 700 kg was met using light materials: extruded aluminum for the chassis (40% lighter than an identical steel chassis) and thermoplastic for the body. The fact that both of these materials are easily recycled was another advantage.

To eliminate a few more grams, the body parts were designed to be highly functional and passenger compartment features were kept to a strict minimum. For this reason the dashboard controls resemble those found on motorcycles. Side windows, along with

Pininfarina Ethos 1992

ENGINE
Type: 2-stroke, in-line 3-cylinder, direct fuel injection.
Displacement: 1,200 cc. Bore and stroke: 84 mm x 72 mm.
Horsepower: 95 hp at 5,500 rpm

DIMENSIONS
Length: 3,630 mm; width: 1,660 mm; height: 1,140 mm (1,050 mm without the roof); wheelbase: 2,300 mm; weight: 700 kg

TRANSMISSION
5-speed manual

PERFORMANCE
Maximum speed: not provided

COLLECTION
Pininfarina

their heavy mechanical components, were also eliminated, as was the rigid roof. A flexible fabric roof is available for "emergencies." The bucket seats and dashboard instrumentation are waterproof.

The two-stroke Orbital engine was chosen to limit fuel consumption. This engine produces 95 hp, but requires 35% less fuel than the average 1992 subcompact. Its smaller size also provided greater flexibility for the designers. When the Ethos I was presented to the public, its low level of polluting emissions meant that the car could be classed as an Ultra-Low-Emission vehicle under California's extremely stringent anti-pollution standards.

47.

Pininfarina Ethos II 1993

THE ETHOS II IS AN EXTENSION OF THE ORIGINAL ETHOS, AND HAS KEPT 70% of its predecessor's modular components. From the green leisure-oriented sport model unveiled 10 months earlier, Pininfarina moved on to a personal automobile intended for such mundane tasks as getting to the office, the factory or the grocery store. While this vehicle was to provide functional transportation, it was not, strictly speaking, a family car.

The Ethos II was designed as an elegant two-seater coupe, with the same front end and curved sides as the original green sport model. Electrically operated side windows and a roof provided the occupants with greater comfort. The dashboard was the same as the one in the Ethos.

Despite the changes, the Ethos II was only 30 kg heavier than the earlier model – a reasonable increase considering its greater comfort. By substituting a 2-cylinder Orbital engine for the 3-cylinder powerplant found in the Ethos, the designers managed to limit the weight gain.

Nonetheless, the Ethos II had to meet the same environmental concerns. For this reason it used similar construction methods. A body of recyclable thermoplastic rode on a modular chassis of extruded aluminum. The new model used narrower tires than the original Ethos, with lower rolling resistance.

Despite its low displacement – barely 800 cc – the engine provided 55 horsepower. The low weight and efficient body design – a drag coefficient of 0.19 and a perfectly flat undercarriage – allowed the car to accelerate from 0 to 100 km/h in only 13 seconds. Another remarkable fact: the Ethos II engine provides almost twice the fuel efficiency of the Geo Metro, although the Metro is the Canadian fuel economy leader for 1995. At a constant speed of 90 km/h, the Ethos II consumes 2.1 litres/100 km, compared to the Metro's 5 litres.

To accommodate North American driving habits, Pininfarina also considered building an Ethos II with an automatic transmission and a supercharged version of the 2-cylinder Orbital engine.

Pininfarina Ethos II 1993

ENGINE
Type: 2-stroke, in-line 2-cylinder, direct fuel injection.
Displacement: 800 cc. Bore and stroke: 84 mm x 72 mm.
Horsepower: 55 hp at 5,500 rpm

DIMENSIONS
Length: 3,975 mm; width: 1,660 mm; height: 1,150 mm; wheelbase: 2,300 mm; weight: 730 kg

TRANSMISSION
5-speed manual

PERFORMANCE
Estimated maximum speed: 200 km/h

COLLECTION
Pininfarina

48.

Pininfarina Ethos III EV 1995

THE ETHOS III EV WAS UNVEILED IN JANUARY 1995 AT THE LOS ANGELES Auto Show. This is the second-largest such event in the United States after the Detroit Auto Show, which takes place at the same time. Pininfarina's choice of Los Angeles was no accident, since California has the strictest anti-pollution regulations in the United States. As of 1998, the state will require all large automakers to market a "clean" car, that is, a Zero-Emission Vehicle (ZEV), that produces no polluting gases.

Pininfarina Ethos III EV 1995

ENGINE
Type: Electric, DC with permanent magnets.
Power : 55.2 kW
DIMENSIONS
Length: 3,365 mm; width: 1,690 mm; height: 1,470 mm;
wheelbase: 2,300 mm; weight: 1,050 kg
TRANSMISSION
Electronic control system
PERFORMANCE
Maximum speed: 161 km/h
COLLECTION
Pininfarina

The Ethos III EV is the fourth vehicle produced as part of the Ethos project, which takes a totally new approach to the environmental problems posed by the automobile.

The EV model is in fact an improved Ethos III. The hatchback-style body has been modified slightly to meet American safety regulations (the bumpers have been altered, for example). Pininfarina has also attempted to make the vehicle more attractive to the Americain driver. The passenger compartment has a more conservative look, and can hold five passengers (rather than the six that could fit into the Ethos III). A fixed steering wheel has replaced the moveable one found in the earlier car and the dashboard now hides dual airbags, a safety feature that is both increasingly common and increasingly in demand in the United States. The rear hatch has a third stop light set above the rear-window wiper, and there is even a mounting plate for a standard North American license plate.

In France, this vehicle is called a monospace; in North America we call it a minivan. The principle is simple: combine the passenger compartment with the space usually reserved for luggage in order to create a multipurpose vehicle. The user can simply modify the vehicle according to the number of passengers to be transported or the amount of material to be carried. It is more than a car, but not quite a van.

Each year, these multipurpose minivans take a greater share of the market, so Pininfarina decided to present such a vehicle as part of its Ethos project.

Like the two Ethos vehicles unveiled in 1992 and 1993, the Ethos III combines elegance, innovation, environmental considerations, driving pleasure, lightness, safety and recyclable components. The vehicle is far from the contemporary minivan epitomized by the Dodge Caravan, however. On the contrary, in size it is not very different from the two previous Ethos models. Built on the same wheelbase, the Ethos III is actually the shortest of the three. It is only 30 mm wider, and weighs only 80 kg more than the sport model.

Nonetheless, the vehicle was designed to transport up to six adults and is powered by the 3-cylinder Orbital engine that was used in the original Ethos.

Ethos III 1994.

The Ethos III is, in fact, the length of a contemporary city car such as the 1995 Geo Metro, and as wide and high as an average sedan.

The body, which has some of the characteristics of the other two Ethos models, has a drag coefficient of only 0.31 – the same as the Ford Contour – despite its higher, more vanlike appearance.

True to its initial concept, the Ethos III body is made of thermoplastic panels mounted on a modular chassis of extruded aluminum. The low-rolling-resistance tires are by Goodyear. In this case, however, the manual gearshift has been replaced by a continuously variable automatic transmission, like that used in the 1960s by Holland's Daf and more recently by Japan's Subaru Justy.

Interior of Ethos III 1994.

The aluminum chassis of the Ethos III EV.

To provide greater interior space, the 2-stroke Orbital engine has been mounted further forward. The result is an extremely spacious passenger compartment with a perfectly flat floor. The three front seats can be adjusted forward and back, while the three seat backs of the rear seat can be folded down independently. The central seats are slightly off-centre, providing a better view for the middle passenger in the rear.

The driving position is also adjustable. Instead of a traditional dashboard, a horizontal aluminum tube is mounted ahead of the front-seat passengers. An adjustable module holding the steering wheel and the dashboard instruments (the same ones found on the other Ethos models) may be moved in front of any of the three front bucket seats. This makes the Ethos III instantly adaptable to the local driving environment – a practical solution for the British driver crossing the Channel, for example. This flexibility may also be helpful in difficult parking situations.

The Ethos III EV is one of tomorrow's clean cars ("EV" stands for Electric Vehicle). The extremely short hood hides an electric engine that supplies power to the front wheels. It uses energy from a series of lead-acid batteries stored in three battery boxes. Two of these boxes are found under the front seats, while one is situated under the trunk floor. Baggage space in the Ethos III EV is almost as large as in the earlier model.

The batteries add significant weight to the EV. The Ethos III weighed less than 800 kg, but the EV weighs in at 324 kg more. The EV has a range of 161 kilometres at a constant speed of 80 km/h, and the car can reach a maximum speed of 100 km/h in 11.3 seconds.

The beauty of this particular "clean car," compared to many others, is the speed with which it can be recharged. The batteries can be recharged to 50% capacity in less than 20 minutes, while 30 minutes is enough to bring them up to 99% capacity. The batteries themselves will last for 100,000 km.

The Ethos III EV was designed specifically for the California market. It was developed and built by Pininfarina's American design studio in Troy, Michigan, in partnership with Unique Mobility of Golden, Colorado, a company specializing in the development of components for electric cars.

Like the previous Ethos model, the Ethos III EV has a body of recyclable plastic over an aluminum chassis.

Biographies

Walter Owen BENTLEY
1888-1971

From earliest childhood, Walter Owen Bentley wanted to be an engineer. W. O., as he was known, first worked with his brother Henry in London as a dealer in French automobiles. In 1914, he joined the British navy and worked in its air service, where he attracted attention for his creations, which included the radial engine used in the Sopwith Camel aircraft. In 1920, he began to build the automobiles that bore his name. Bentleys made a reputation for themselves on the racing circuit, taking the Le Mans 24-hour race five times between 1924 and 1930. In 1933, his company fell victim to the Depression and was taken over by Rolls-Royce. In 1935, Bentley left the company to join Lagonda, where he was technical director until 1947. He then moved on to Armstrong-Siddeley, another small British manufacturer of luxury cars.

Karl BENZ
1844-1929

Karl Benz was born in Karlsruhe, Germany, and showed a keen interest in technology at an early age. He entered the Technische Hochschule at age 16, where he was greatly impressed by Professor Ferdinand Redtenbacher's pronouncement that a new power source, the liquid-fuel engine, would soon supplant the steam engine. Later, Benz worked in a locomotive manufacturing plant, which he left in 1866, three years before the arrival of a new chief engineer by the name of Gottlieb Daimler. In 1871, Benz founded his own business in Mannheim, the Rheinische Gasmotorenfabrik, and began developing internal-combustion engines. His motor-tricycle was the first in a series of vehicles he produced. By the end of the nineteenth century, he had manufactured some two thousand automobiles. Three years before his death, his company merged with Daimler, manufacturer of the Mercedes.

Gordon Miller BUEHRIG
1904-1990

Engineer and designer, Gordon Buehrig conceived the unorthodox look of the 1935 Cord 810/812. The car was so unusual that Buehrig took the precaution of applying for a patent to protect his creation, which was the first American automobile with front-wheel drive and an independent front suspension. According to its creator, it represented "a new, original and decorative automobile design".[1] Before moving on to work for Erret Loban Cord, Buehrig had been a designer for General Motors. In 1929, the president of Duesenberg hired him to design the coachwork for the first Duesenberg J models. Gordon Buehrig also designed the impressive 1935 Auburn 851 for Erret Cord.

Ettore Arco Isidoro BUGATTI
1881-1947

The son of a cabinetmaker, Italian Ettore Bugatti clearly inherited considerable artistic talent. In 1899, he joined Prinetti and Stucchi as an apprentice. Two years later, he unveiled his first automobile, built for Count Gulinelli. Bugatti was not yet 20 when he moved to Alsace to work for Baron de Dietrich. Following a disagreement, the arrangement ended, and in 1904 Bugatti went to work for Mathis in Strasbourg. In 1907, he was in Cologne as chief engineer for Deutz, and in 1909, he founded a company of his own in Mulhouse, not far from Strasbourg. Two years later, he designed the "Baby" Peugeot for the French automaker. His employees referred to him as "le Patron". His career was marked by a long succession of innovations and the unveiling of a series of breathtaking automobiles. The most amazing of these was undoubtedly the Royale, also called the 41. The accidental death of his only son Jean in 1939 was a blow from which Bugatti never fully recovered.

1   Ludvigsen and Burgess-Wise 1979, p. 54

Jean BUGATTI
1909-1939

Born on January 15, Jean was the son of Ettore Bugatti. He became production supervisor at his father's car factory in 1929. A talented designer, he was responsible for such masterpieces as the Royale Napoleon coupe, the 57 Atlantic, the 50T and the Type 55, among others. He soon become his father's principal colleague. Since Ettore was spending more and more time in Paris and in Belgium, where he hoped to establish a second Molsheim works, he appointed Jean as head of the factory. Gradually, Jean's influence became apparent in the automobiles produced at Molsheim, but he died before the first model to fully incorporate his ideas could be marketed. Jean Bugatti was killed during a test run in August 1939.

Walter Percy CHRYSLER
1875-1940

A native of Wamego, Kansas, Walter Chrysler at first followed in the footsteps of his father and elder brother by going to work for the Union Pacific Railroad. He rose through the ranks of the railroad industry to become manager of the American Locomotive Company in Pittsburgh. In 1912,[1] he left to join Buick. In 1920, when he was president of Buick and first vice-president of General Motors, the Willys-Overland company asked him to save the faltering firm. He left GM and succeeded in getting Willys-Overland back on an even keel. Starting in 1921, he applied his energy to rescuing another car manufacturer, the Maxwell-Chalmers Corporation, where he quickly took control. In 1924, following restructuring, the company launched the first car bearing the Chrysler name, the Chrysler B-70. The next year, the company was renamed Chrysler Corporation. Walter Chrysler died on August 18, 1940, after a long illness.

Erret Loban CORD
1894-1974

Erret Loban Cord was born on a farm in Missouri. At the age of 30, he was a dealer for Moon automobiles in Chicago. Business was booming, and he gained a reputation as the country's top car salesman.[2] The Auburn Automobile Company invited Cord to join its staff in order to reorganize the company's troubled finances. Within a year, Cord owned Auburn, which was now making money. Before long, he controlled an empire that included Duesenberg, American Airlines, Stinson Aviation, the Lycoming auto engine firm, several coachbuilding shops and the New York Shipbuilding Corporation. A tireless worker, Cord was also a chronic gambler. In 1929, he established the car company bearing his name, but that same year the stock market crash put the Auburn-Cord-Duesenberg automobile conglomerate in jeopardy. In 1937, after the Cord factory ceased operation, Erret Cord became interested in two nascent technologies: radio and television.

André DUBONNET
1897-1980

Grandson of the creator of the Dubonnet aperitif, André Dubonnet served in the French air force where he rapidly made a name for himself. He then drove in various motor racing events. At Monza and Le Mans, and in the Targa Florio, among others, Dubonnet drove his Hispano-Suiza with such elan that Ettore Bugatti was impressed enough to hire him. A man of immense creativity, Dubonnet had always dreamed of building his own automobile. In the 1920s and 1930s, Dubonnet had Nieuport produce coachwork for a Hispano-Suiza, built some original chassis, marketed a new, independent front suspension system, and had at least three cars built bearing the trademark of the leaping cat. During the 1960s, Dubonnet sat on the board of directors of the French carmaker Simca. He died in the winter of 1980 from complications arising from a car accident three years earlier.

Piero DUSIO
1903-1956

Before World War II, Piero Dusio was the Italian amateur auto racing champion. An experienced businessman, he built his first sports car in 1939, but the war prevented the start of production. In 1946, Dusio used the fortune he amassed during the war to found the Cisitalia company in Turin. He then undertook production of sport coupes – including the famous 202 with coachwork by Pinin Farina – and played an major role in the world of auto racing. He asked Dante Giacosa to create a modular chassis for a single-seater using a Fiat 1100 engine. In 1947, he also launched a monotype championship (the "formula Cisitalia" no less!) that lasted only one season. He invested an enormous sum of money in the development of the 360 Grand Prix model. Bankrupt in 1948, Dusio left Italy for Argentina, where he took part in dictator Juan Perón's plan to create a national automobile company.

2   Rosenbusch in Chrysler/Bailey 1994, p. 13.

3   Tubbs 1978 p. 80.

George EYSTON
1897 - 197?

A lanky Briton, George Eyston was greatly impressed by Ralph de Palma's performance at the 1921 Le Mans 24-hour race. Two years later, Eyston found himself driving a Sunbeam single-seater racing car and went on to make his name as a record-breaker. From 1927 to 1954, he took part in countless projects to set new speed records. While he was perhaps not the most famous of British record-holders, he was definitely the longest-lasting.[4] At the end of World War I, Eyston was awarded the British Military Cross and, after World War II, the Order of the British Empire and the French Legion of Honour.

Enzo FERRARI
1898-1988

Enzo Ferrari was born in the northern Italian city of Modena on February 18, 1898. The young Enzo had three passions: opera, journalism and, above all, car racing. He enlisted in the Italian army during World War I and after being demobilized, went to work for the CMN automobile company. In 1920, he moved to Alfa-Romeo and in 1929, as head of the racing team, he founded the Ferrari Scuderia. In 1938, he left Alfa-Romeo to establish Auto Avio Costruzioni in Modena and then in 1943 moved the company to Maranello. In 1940, he had created his first car, known simply as the 815. The first automobile to bear the name Ferrari, the model 125, was launched in 1947. Ferrari entered his cars in the Le Mans 24-hour race for the first time in 1949. In 1952, when the great Alberto Ascari won a first Grand Prix world championship for Ferrari, a legend was born. In 1969, in order to save his company, Ferrari was obliged to transfer a large part of its assets to Fiat. He died on August 14, 1988.

Jim HALL
1935 -

James Ellis Hall was born in Abilene, Texas, on July 23, 1935, the youngest of three children. His father had major holdings in an oil company. Hall earned a degree in mechanical engineering at CalTech in Pasadena, California, in 1957; three years earlier, however, he had already had his first taste of motor racing. He began his driving career in the late 1950s. In 1961, he created the first Chaparral.

Camille JENATZY
1868-1913

Camille Jenatzy was born in Brussels[5] of Polish parents.[6] At an early age, he developed a passion for racing and sporting events and also enjoyed tinkering with bicycles. At the turn of the century, he worked as an engineer for the Compagnie internationale des transports automobiles de Paris, a manufacturer of electric carriages. He first raced in 1898 and that same year achieved notoriety for his challenge to Count Chasseloup-Laubat. He then began a racing career that saw him drive for the Mercedes, Pipe and Mors stables. He met an untimely death in 1913 during a party at his hunting lodge in the Ardennes. The man nicknamed "the Red Devil" for his red hair and flamboyant personality was accidently shot dead by one of his friends.

Anthony LAGO
1893-1960

A native of Venice, Anthony Lago trained as an engineer at the Politecnico di Milano. He moved to London in the early 1920s and worked for Isotta-Fraschini. He fought in the Italian army in World War I. Later, he became director of Wilson Self-Changing Gear Ltd. Lago was also a driver for the British firm Armstrong-Siddeley. In 1933, he became the director of the Talbot factory in Suresnes, France, part of the Sunbeam-Talbot-Darracq consortium (STD).[7] When STD collapsed two years later, Lago took charge of the French factory of the Rootes group, which had acquired STD's assets. Until 1959, he made some of France's most beautiful cars and played a major role in the world of Grand Prix racing. Talbot-Lago was bought by Simca in 1960.

Hans LEDWINKA
1878-1967

A native of Klosterneuberg, near Vienna, Hans Ledwinka was not yet 20 years old when he started at the Nesselsdorfer company. For almost 70 years, he worked in the auto industry, mainly at Nesselsdorfer, which later became Tatra. He also worked at Friedmann (1902-1905) and Styer (1916-1921). During World War II, the Tatra factory produced war materials; although apolitical, Ledwinka became director of a German defence programme, which, in the eyes of the Czechoslovak Communist Party that came to power after the war, warranted his imprisonment and subsequent exile.

4   Cutter and Fendell 1973, p. 194.

5   Ward ed. 1974, Vol. 10, p. 1,091.

6   Jamais-Contente/Tavard n.d. p. 3.

7   Aceti 1979, p. 40.

William LYONS
1901-1985
Born in Blackpool, England, William Lyons first worked for the Crosley company. He then sold automobiles before entering into a partnership with William Walmsley to found Swallow Sidecar in 1922, the company that was later to become Jaguar Cars. For Lyons, the tragic accident at the 1955 Le Mans race was compounded by the death of his only son in a traffic accident while on his way to meet him at the famous racing venue. In 1965, Lyons merged Jaguar with the British Motor Corporation (BMC) group, where he remained head of the company until 1972.

Louis MEYER
1904-1943
American racing-car driver Louis Meyer was the son of Edward Meyer, a turn-of-the-century cycling champion. He was the first driver to win the Indianapolis 500 three times. He first drove the Indy 500 in 1927 and made his last appearance there in 1939.

Harry Armenius MILLER
1875-1943
Harry Miller's father was of German origin and spelled his name Mueller, but Harry preferred the Americanized version. He struck out on his own at an early age, rather than take the path planned for him by his parents. At the age of 13, he became an apprentice mechanic and was soon specializing in carburetors. In 1909, he marketed a spark plug of his own design, followed by the Master carburetor. On the eve of World War I, he was already running his own piston works, which were among the first in the North America to use aluminum. At this same time, he began providing custom engine modifications. After the war, he produced high-performance racing engines and began building race cars in 1923.

Paul PANHARD
1881-1969
In 1909, Paul Panhard joined the firm founded by his uncle, René Panhard, and Émile Levassor. He gained a thorough understanding of the company by working in each of its departments. He was conscripted in 1914 and became general manager upon his return two years later. A lawyer by training, he surrounded himself with a team of competent engineers to make up for his lack of technical knowledge. In 1937, he appointed his son Jean, trained at the École Polytechnique, as Panhard's technical director. Some believe that his conservative outlook slowed the company's development. At any rate, in 1955 he handed over control of Panhard to Citroën after spending a half century at its helm. He died in March 1969 at the age of 88.

Battista PININFARINA
1893-1966
The 10th of 11 children in a peasant family, Battista Farina arrived in Turin at the end of the last century. He was nicknamed "Pinin", which in the Piedmont dialect meant that he was the youngest son of a large family.[8] In 1904, at age 11, he began working in his elder brother's body shop. Twenty-five years later, when he was a master coachbuilder, he set up his own company in Turin – the Carrozzeria Pinin Farina. He would have many great achievements, including the Lancia Dilambda and Astura, the Cisitalia 202, the Ferrari 212 and 375MM, the Morris 1100 and Austin A40, and the Alfa-Romeo Giulietta. In 1958, the company moved to new premises in the Turin suburb of Grugliasco. In 1961, a decree of Italian President Giovanni Gronchi authorized a change of family name to "Pininfarina", a change that was also applied to the company. In 1963, Battista Pininfarina was awarded the Legion of Honour by French President Charles de Gaulle. He died three years later after a brief illness.

Sergio PININFARINA
1926 -
Sergio Pininfarina was born in Turin on September 8, 1926. A mechanical engineer by training, he spent brief periods studying in England and the United States before joining the family firm in the early 1950s. Convinced of the importance of aerodynamics, in 1965 he began a study to determine the feasibility of building a wind tunnel for full-size models. His wind tunnel was completed in 1972. In the meantime, in 1966, Sergio had found himself at the head of the company following the death of his father Battista. In 1951, he married Giorgia Gianolio, and they had three children: Lorenza, Andrea and Paolo.

8   Pininfarina/Merlin 1980, p. 11.

Ferdinand PORSCHE
1875-1951

Of Austrian origin, Ferdinand Porsche was born in Bohemia. In 1896, he completed his first automobile, which was equipped with two front-powered wheels. The vehicle had been commissioned by Ludwig Lohner, a Viennese builder of horse-drawn carriages, who hoped to move into automobile manufacturing. Next, Porsche worked for the Austrian companies Styer and Austro-Daimler. He then emigrated to Germany, settling in Stuttgart in 1923. He founded a design office in 1930 and carried out commissions for Zündapp, Mercedes-Benz, Auto Union and Cisitalia before finally creating the first car to bear his name, just after World War II. Of course, Ferdinand Porsche also designed the famous Volkswagen Beetle, which dates from 1936. Porsche died on January 30, 1951.

Ferry PORSCHE
1909 -

Born on September 19, 1909, at Wiener Neustadt,[9] Ferry Porsche was the son of Ferdinand Porsche. He was one of the first employees at his father's design studio. Following Ferdinand's death in 1951, Ferry took over the family business. His son Ferdinand Alexander, known as Butzi, designed the body for the celebrated Porsche 911.

Edmund RUMPLER
1872-1940

Edmund Rumpler was born in Bohemia, then a province of the Austro-Hungarian Empire. In 1897, he began working in the auto industry at Nesselsdorfer. After a brief stint at Daimler, he worked for Adler from 1903 to 1907. Rumpler then became deeply involved in the aviation industry, where he was responsible for the Taube monoplane. One of the German planes most feared by Allied forces during World War I, the Taube symbolized the Kaiser's superiority in fighter aircraft. Barred from the aviation industry after the war, Rumpler returned to the automobile and presented his first car at the 1921 Berlin show. He continued building cars bearing his name until 1926.

Preston Thomas TUCKER
1903-1956

Tucker was born in Capac, Michigan, on September 21, 1903. While still a boy, he worked as an errand boy at Cadillac. During the 1920s, he worked on an assembly line at Ford. Later, he was a salesman for Studebaker and then Dodge, before becoming a regional manager for Pierce-Arrow. In 1935, he teamed up with Harry Miller to build racing cars; he already dreamed of producing his own automobile. At the end of the 1930s, he established Tucker Aviation Corporation to build a high-speed armoured car capable of 187 km/h and equipped with a unique, multidirectional gun turret. The American Army kept the turret design but considered the vehicle to be unnecessarily powerful. In 1944, Tucker began his automobile project in a workshop next to his house in Ypsilanti, Michigan. He died in 1956 before he could follow through on plans for a second car, an elegant Tucker coupe designed by Alexis de Sakhnoffsky.

Gabriel VOISIN
1880-1973

The oldest of four children, Gabriel Voisin spent his childhood in the Lyons region, developing a passion for kites. Later, while studying architecture in Paris, he discovered aeronautics. After a brief association with Louis Blériot, Voisin and his brother Charles formed an aircraft manufacturing company. Gabriel was severely shaken by his brother's accidental death, but World War I revitalized his business. In 1919, he turned to automobile manufacturing. The nonconformist, impulsive and solitary Voisin produced a series of extravagant, even fantastic, automobiles. In 1937, a lack of money prompted Voisin to quit his company, which survived for two more years under new management. World War II saw Voisin's return to aviation. At age 72, he retired to Spain, where he worked on the development of an inexpensive minicar known as the Biscuter.

9   Porsche/Porsche n.d., p. 13.

Selected bibliography

GENERAL BOOKS

ACETI, Enrica. *Les belles voitures des années folles*. Paris: Atlas, 1979. 191 pp.

Automobile Manufacturers Association. *Automobiles of America*. Detroit: Wayne State University Press, 1968. 269 pp.

BARKER, Ronald, and Douglas B. TUBBS. *Automobiles and Automobiling*. New York: Bonanza Books, 1965. 209 pp.

BEATTIE, Ian. *The Complete Book of Automobile Body Design*. Sparkford, England: Haynes, 1977. 143 pp.

BELLU, René. *Toutes les voitures françaises 1939*. Lausanne: Edita-Vilo, 1982. 133 pp.

BELLU, Serge. *Le sang bleu*. Paris: EPA, 1978. 241 pp.

BOCHROCH, Albert R. *American Automobile Racing*. New York: Penguin Books, 1974. 260 pp.

BROWN, Peter, ed. *America at the Wheel – 100 Years of the Automobile in America*. Detroit: Automotive News, 1993. 216 pp.

BURGESS-WISE, David. *Veteran and Vintage Cars*. London: Hamlyn, 1970. 159 pp.

BÜSCHI, Hans U., et al. *Catalogue 93 de la Revue automobile*. Bern: Hallwag, 1993. 588 pp.

CASUCCI, Piero. *Racing Cars*. Chicago: Rand McNally, 1981. 256 pp.

——. *Classic Cars*. New York: Rand McNally, 1978. 287 pp.

COTTON, Michael. *The Le Mans 24-hour Race*. Wellingborough, England: Patrick Stephens, 1989. 152 pp.

COULTER, Jeremy, ed. *The World's Great Cars*. Secaucus, N.J.: Chartwell Books, 1989. 416 pp.

CULSHAW, David, and Peter HORROBIN. *The Complete Catalogue of British Cars*. New York: William Morrow, 1974. 510 pp.

CUTTER, Robert, and Bob FENDELL. *Encyclopedia of Auto Racing Greats*. Englewood Cliffs, N.J.: Prentice-Hall, 1973. 675 pp.

DANIELS, Ted E., ed. *75 Years of the Indianapolis 500*. Indianapolis: Indianapolis Star, n.d.

DUMONT, Pierre, et al. *Automobiles and Automobiling*. New York: Bonanza Books, 1965. 209 pp.

FERSEN, Hans-Heinrich von. *Autos in Deutschland 1920-1939*. Stuttgart: Motorbuch Verlag, 1967. 360 pp.

Fifty Years of American Automobiles: 1939-1989. New York: Beekman House, 1989. 720 pp.

FLAMMANG, James M. *Standard Catalog of Imported Cars, 1946-1990*. Iola: Krause Publications, 1992. 704 pp.

FOX, Jack C. *The Indianapolis 500*. Cleveland: World Publishing, 1967. 300 pp.

GABBARD, Alex. *Vintage and Historic Racing Cars*. Tucson: HP Books, 1986. 192 pp.

GEORGANO, G. N. *The Encyclopedia of Motor Sport*. New York: Viking, 1971, pp. 539-541.

GEORGANO, G. N., ed. *The Complete Encyclopedia of Motorcars – 1885 to the Present*. New York: E.P. Dutton, 1973. 751 pp.

Grand Prix Molson du Canada. *Guide média Grand Prix Molson du Canada 1991*, 1991. 151 pp.

——. *Media Information: Grand Prix Molson du Canada 1990*, 1990. 109 pp.

GUICHARD, Ami, ed. *L'Année automobile 1980-81*. Lausanne: Edita, 1980. 253 pp.

GUNNELL, John A. *Standard Catalog of American Cars, 1946-1975*. Iola: Krause Publications, 1982. 736 pp.

HODGES, David. *A-Z of Formula Racing Cars*. Bideford, England: Bay View Books, 1990. 279 pp.

HOWARD, Geoffrey. *Automobile Aerodynamics*. London: Osprey, 1986. 191 pp.

HUGO, Peter. *Private Motor Car Collections of Great Britain*. London: Dalton Watson, 1973. 207 pp.

ICKX, Jacques. *Ainsi naquit l'automobile*. Lausanne: Edita-Vilo, 1971. 244 pp.

KIMES, Beverly Rae, ed. *Great Cars & Great Marques.* Princeton: Automobile Quarterly, Inc., 1976. 239 pp.

KIMES, Beverly Rae, and Henry Austin CLARK, Jr. *Standard Catalog of American Cars, 1805-1942.* Iola: Krause Publications, 1985. 1,536 pp.

KING, Peter. *The Motor Men.* London: Quiller Press, 1989, 168 pp.

LANGWORTH, Richard M. *The New Complete Book of Collectible Cars, 1930-1990.* Lincolnwood, Illinois: Publications International, 1992. 576 pp.

LAWRENCE, Mike. *Directory of Grand Prix Cars, 1945-65.* Bourne End, England: Aston Publications, 1989. 264 pp.

LUDVIGSEN, Karl, and David BURGESS-WISE. *The Complete Encyclopedia of the American Automobile.* Secaucus, N.J.: Chartwell Books, 1979. 191 pp.

LURANI, Giovanni. *La fabuleuse histoire des Mille Miglia.* Lausanne: Edita-Vilo, 1981. 207 pp.

MOLONEY, James. *Encyclopedia of American Cars, 1930-1942.* Sarasota: Crestline Publishing, 1977. 383 pp.

MORRISON, Ian. *Guinness Motor Racing Records, Facts and Champions.* Enfield, England: Guinness Publishing, 1989. 192 pp.

Motor Vehicle Manufacturers Association of the United States, Inc., *World Motor Vehicle Data, 1992.* Detroit: MVMA, 1992. 354 pp.

Musée français de l'automobile. Paris: Iris, 1975. 71 pp.

NAUL, G. Marshall. *The Specification Book for US Cars, 1920-1929.* Osceola: Motorbooks International, 1978. 325 pp.

NESBITT, Dick. *American Automobile Design, 1930-1980.* Skokie, Illinois: Publications International, 1985. 64 pp.

NORBYE, Jan P. *The Complete History of the German Car – 1886 to the Present.* New York: Portland House, 1987. 239 pp.

NYE, Doug. *History of the Grand Prix Car, 1945-65.* Richmond, England: Hazleton Publishing, 1993. 288 pp.

———. *History of the Grand Prix Car, 1966-91.* Richmond, England: Hazleton Publishing, 1992. 352 pp.

OLYSLAGER, Piet. *Les automobiles dans le monde de 1770 à aujourd'hui.* Paris: RST, 1967. 255 pp.

PLUMMER, John. *Best Loved Cars of the World.* Secaucus, N.J.: Chartwell Books, 1979. 96 pp.

PORÁZIK, Juraj. *Motor Cars, 1770-1940.* Leicester: Galley Press, 1981. 224 pp.

ROGLIATTI, Gianni. *Les plus belles voitures d'époque.* Paris: Deux Coqs d'Or, 1971. 318 pp.

ROSINSKI, José, et al. *Guide Sport-Auto Formule 1 90.* Special issue no. 12, 1990. 106 pp.

ROUSSEAU, Jacques, and Jean-Paul CARON. *Guide de l'automobile française.* N.p.: Solar, 1993. 589 pp.

SÉCLIER, Philippe, et al. *Auto Hebdo – 1990 Une saison de sport automobile.* Special issue no. 13. 162 pp.

SETRIGHT, L.J.K. *The Designers – Great Automobiles and the Men Who Made Them.* Chicago: Follett, 1976. 199 pp.

STEIN, Ralph. *Les voitures célèbres.* Paris: Planète, 1970. 252 pp.

TAYLOR, Rich. *Indy: Seventy-five Years of Racing's Greatest Spectacle.* New York: St. Martin's Press, 1991. pp. 58-64.

TRAGATSCH, Erwin. *Le dictionnaire Marabout des voitures de sport et de compétition.* Verviers, Belgium: Gérard, 1971. 3 vols.

TUBBS, D. B. *Art and the Automobile.* New York: Grosset & Dunlap, 1978. 144 pp.

VANDERVEEN, Bart H., ed. *British Cars of the Late Thirties.* London: Frederick Warne. 1973. 80 pp.

WARD, Ian, ed. *The World of Automobiles.* New York: Columbia House, 1974. 22 vols.

WHYTE, Andrew. *A Touch of Class.* London: Octopus Books, 1985. 160 pp.

WOOD, Jonathan. *Great Marques of Germany.* New York: Gallery Books, 1985. 224 pp.

BOOKS, ARTICLES AND MEDIA INFORMATION BY MARQUE

ALFA-ROMEO

GARY, Pierre. "Alfa Romeo 6C 1750 Grand Sport 1930 : sur les traces des Mille Miglia". *Auto Passion,* no. 55 (October 1991), pp. 46-56.

HULL, Peter. *Alfa Romeo.* New York: Ballantine Books, 1971. 157 pp.

MOITY, Christian. "Alfa Romeo : 4 fois 20 ans !". *Auto Passion.* no. 38 (August 1990), pp. 72-80.

ORSINI, Luigi. "The Dynasty Begins – Enzo Ferrari's Scuderia Days". *Automobile Quarterly,* vol. 17, no. 2 (1979), pp. 116-131.

STEIN, Ralph. "1750 Alfa and the Giulietta". *Automobile Quarterly,* vol. 1, no. 1 (1962), pp. 64-67.

VASSAL, Jacques. "Les bonnes feuilles du trèfle". *Auto Passion*, no. 56 (October 1991), pp. 35-38.

AUTO UNION

BAMSEY, Ian. *Auto Union V16 Supercharged – A Technical Appraisal*. Sparkford, England: Haynes, 1990. 96 pp.

MERLIN, Didier. *Audi : une tradition sportive*. Lausanne: Edita, 1981. 109 pp.

MOITY, Christian. "Un titan d'argent". *Automobiles classiques*, no. 12 (February/March 1986), pp. 50-57.

AUBURN

KIMES, Beverly R. "The Glorious Boattail". *Automobile Quarterly*, vol. 16, no. 1 (1978), pp. 42-61.

LORRIMER, Michael. "Auburn: The Second Time Around". *Automobile Quarterly*, vol. 6, no. 3 (1968), pp. 309-313.

BENTLEY

ADAMS, John, and Ray ROBERTS. *A Pride of Bentley*. Secaucus, N.J.: Chartwell Books, 1978. 219 pp.

POSTHUMUS, Cyril. *Bentley – Toute l'histoire*. Paris: EPA, 1983. Not paginated.

BMW

NORBYE, Jan P. *BMW: Bavaria's Driving Machine*. Skokie, Illinois: Publications International, 1984. 256 pp.

SCHNITZLER, Winfred M. *Histoire des grandes marques : BMW*. Verviers, Belgium: Marabout Service, 1969. 222 pp.

SCHRADER, Halwart. *BMW: A History*. Toronto: Clarke Irwin, 1979. 392 pp.

SEIFERT, Eberhard. *The Complete History of BMW*. Milan: Automobilia, 1980. Not paginated.

SIMSA, Paul. *BMW : la suprématie technologique automobile*. Paris: EPA, 1984. 202 pp.

SLONIGER, Jerry. "BMW: A Sporting History". *Automobile Quarterly*, vol. 6, no. 3 (1968), pp. 314-329.

BOWES

Automobile Quarterly, vol. 33, no. 1 (1994), pp. 74-75.

FOX, Jack C. *The Indianapolis 500*. Cleveland: World Publishing, 1967. 300 pp.

BUGATTI

AUBERT, Philippe. *Les Bugatti*. Paris: J.-C. Lattès, 1981. 278 pp.

BARKER, Ronald. *Bugatti*. New York: Ballantine Books, 1971. 157 pp.

BORGÉ, Jacques, and Nicolas VIASNOFF. *La Bugatti*. Paris: Balland, 1977. 187 pp.

CONWAY, Hugh, and Maurice SAUZAY. *Bugatti Magnum*. Osceola: Motorbooks International, 1989. 559 pp.

KESTLER, Paul. *The Complete Book of Bugatti*. Milan: Automobilia, 1980. Not paginated.

LAINE, Didier. "Bugatti : le style du prince Jean". *Auto-Moto-Rétro*, August 1986, pp. 58-72.

SAUZAY, Maurice. "Chef-d'œuvre". *Automobiles classiques*, no. 37 (April/May 1990), pp. 78-87.

——. *Guide Bugatti – Tous les modèles de 1910 à nos jours*. [Paris]: EPA, 1992. 126 pp.

CADILLAC

HENDRY, Maurice D. Cadillac – *The Complete History*. Kutztown, Pennsylvania: Automobile Quarterly, 1990. 504 pp.

KELLMAN, Jerold L., et al. *Cadillac: Standard of Excellence, 1903-1980*. Skokie, Illinois: Consumer Guide, 1980. 96 pp.

LEROUX, Michel. "Cadillac Eldorado Brougham 1958 : le navire-amiral!". *Auto Passion*, November 1989, pp. 74-82

CASTAGNA

ANSELMI, Angelo T. "Castagna – Raphael of Italian Coachbuilders". *Automobile Quarterly*, vol. 14, no. 1 (1976), pp. 74-91.

CHAPARRAL

CART 1986 Media Guide. Bloomfield Hills: Cart, 1986. 252 pp.

FALCONER, Richard, and Doug NEY. *Chaparral*. Osceola: Motorbooks International, 1992. 208 pp.

HILL, Phil. "Jim Hall and His Chaparrals". *Road & Track*, vol. 31, no. 10 (June 1980), pp. 49-52.

LAMM, John. "Chaparral 2K". *Road & Track*, vol. 31, no. 10 (June 1980), p. 53.

MATTHEWS, Jim. "Indy Cars: The Power before the Horse", *The Canadian Motorsport Annual, 1981-82*. 1982. pp. 9-11.

CHRYSLER

BAILEY, L. Scott, ed. Automobile Quarterly. Kutztown, Pennsylvania: *Automobile Quarterly*, vol. 32, no. 4 (April 1994). 112 pp.

MURRAY, Spence, et al. *Petersen's Complete Book of Plymouth, Dodge, Chrysler.* Los Angeles: Petersen Publishing, 1973. 192 pp.

CISITALIA
See PORSCHE

CORD
LEROUX, Michel. "Cord 810, prématurée... hélas!". *Auto Passion,* no. 27 (September 1989), pp. 50-61.

DUBONNET
DELAROCHE, F. "Dossier Hispano-Suiza". *Auto-Moto-Rétro,* no. 59 (July 1985), pp. 65.

THEVENET, Jean-Paul, and Peter VANN. *Berlinettas.* Osceola: Motorbooks International, pp. 66-70.

USHER, Frederick A. "André Dubonnet – As Supple as a Cat", *Automobile Quarterly,* vol. 24, no. 3 (1986), pp. 272-290.

FERRARI
EATON, Godfrey. *The Complete* Ferrari. Osceola: Motorbooks International, 1989. 376 pp.

FERRARI, Enzo. "My Memoirs". *Automobile Quarterly,* vol. 3, no. 1 (1964), pp. 48-72.

——. *Mes joies terribles.* Verviers, Belgium: Gérard, 1963. 215 pp.

HENRY, Alan. *Ferrari: The Grand Prix Cars.* Richmond, England: Hazleton Publishing, 1989. 352 pp.

MOUNT, Christopher. *Designed for Speed: Three Automobiles by Ferrari.* New York: Museum of Modern Art, 1993. Not paginated.

RANCATI, Gino. *Ferrari: A Memory.* Osceola: Motorbooks International, 1989. 198 pp.

SETRIGHT, Leonard. *Ferrari.* New York: Ballantine Books, 1971. 160 pp.

YATES, Brock. *Enzo Ferrari: The Men, the Cars, the Races.* New York: Doubleday, 1991. 465 pp.

FIAT
DUBARRY, Dominique P. *Fiat.* Paris: EPA, 1986. Not paginated.

SEDGWICK, Michael. *Fiat.* New York: Arco Publishing, 1974. 352 pp.

FIGONI & FALASCHI
BORGESON, Griffith. "Figoni and Falaschi – The Coachbuilder as Sculptor". *Automobile Quarterly,* vol. 20, no. 1 (1982), pp. 48-69.

JAGUAR
BENTLEY, John. *Jaguar Guide.* New York: Sports Car Press, 1957. 127 pp.

BERRY, Robert. *Jaguar – Motor Racing and the Manufacturer.* Tucson: Aztec Corporation, 1978. 94 pages.

MONTAGU OF BEAULIEU, Lord. *Jaguar.* London: Cassell, 1967. 300 pp.

——. *Jaguar – Britain's Fastest Export.* New York: Ballantine Books, 1971. 154 pp.

WHERRY, Joseph H. *Histoire des grandes marques : Jaguar.* Verviers, Belgium: Gérard, 1971. 222 pp.

LA JAMAIS-CONTENTE
LEMAN, Charles. "Toujours plus vite!". *L'Automobile a 100 ans – 1884-1984.* Special issue of *Historia,* no. 449 (April 1984), pp. 34-35.

TAVARD, Christian H. "Il y a 80 ans... le duel pour les 100 km/h". *L'Automobiliste,* no. 52, pp. 3-15.

LAGONDA
VORDERMAN, Don. "Lagonda LG6". *Automobile Quarterly,* vol. 7, no. 3 (1969), pp. 328-333.

LANCIA
FROSTICK, Michael. *Lancia.* London: Dalton Watson, 1976. 208 pp.

GARNIER, Peter. *Lancia.* London: Hamlyn, 1981. 288 pp.

OWEN, David. "Lancia". *Automobile Quarterly,* vol. 12, no. 4 (1974), pp. 340-365.

RAPI, Fabio. "Classic Recalled". *Automobile Quarterly,* vol. 4, no. 3 (1966), pp. 312-313.

MERCEDES-BENZ
CIMAROSTI, Adriano. "Des voitures de course Mercedes qui ont écrit des pages d'histoire". *Mercedes-Benz in aller Welt,* no. 199 (1986), pp. 76-85.

Daimler-Benz AG and Mercedes-Benz Canada. Media information.

GILLIES, Mark. "Black Beauty: Mercedes-Benz SSK". *Supercar Classics,* no. 20 (Winter 1994), pp. 96-105.

JELLINEK-MERCEDES, Guy. *Mon père, Monsieur Mercedes.* Paris: France Empire, 1961. 345 pp.

KIMES, Beverly Rae. *The Star and the Laurel.* Montvale, N.J.: Mercedes-Benz of North America, 1986. 361 pp.

SCOTT-MONCRIEFF, David. *Three-pointed Star – The Story of Mercedes-Benz.* London: Gentry Books, 1979. 434 pp.

STEINWEDEL, Louis-William. *The Mercedes-Benz Story.* Chicago: Rand McNally, 1979. 261 pp.

WEITMANN, Julius. "C-111 Revisited". *Automobile Quarterly,* vol. 17, no. 2, pp. 166-169.

MILLER

BORGESON, Griffith. "A. A. Cadwell: The Angel behind the Golden Sub". *Automobile Quarterly,* vol. 23, no. 1 (1985), pp. 62-64.

——. "The Pre-conquest Millers". *Automobile Quarterly,* vol. 19, no. 1 (1981), pp. 88-103.

DEES, Mark I. "Of Submarines and Time Machines: The Golden Sub Reborn". *Automobile Quarterly,* vol. 23, no. 1 (1985), pp. 58-61, 65-69.

500-mile Race Record Book. Indianapolis: Indianapolis News, 1980, pp. 10-43.

PANHARD

PÉROT, Benoît. *Panhard : la doyenne d'avant-garde.* Paris: EPA, 1979. 493 pp.

——. *Toute l'histoire : Panhard.* Paris: EPA-Automobilia, 1983. Not paginated.

PININFARINA

ALFIERI, Bruno. *Pininfarina.* Paris: EPA, 1982. Not paginated.

BÜSCHI, Hans U., et al. *Catalogue 90 de la Revue automobile.* Bern: Hallwag, 1990, p. 65.

——. *Catalogue 93 de la Revue automobile.* Bern: Hallwag, 1993, p. 73.

FREEMAN, John Whellock. "Pininfarina". *Automobile Quarterly,* vol. 1, no. 4 (1962-1963), pp. 382-395.

MERLIN, Didier. *Pininfarina : Prestige d'une tradition 1930-1980.* Lausanne: Edita, 1980. 244 pp.

Pininfarina SpA. Media information.

Pininfarina : 60 ans de création. Paris: EPA, 1991. 283 pp.

PORSCHE

BOSCHEN, Lothar, and Jürgen BARTH. *The Porsche Book.* Cambridge, England: Patrick Stephens, 1978. 472 pp.

CONRADT, D.-M. *Porsche 356.* Paris: EPA, 1991. 259 pp.

COTTON, Michael. *Classic Porsche Racing Cars.* London: Patrick Stephens, 1988. 151 pp.

FRANKENBERG, Richard von. *Histoire des grandes marques : Porsche.* Verviers, Belgium: Marabout Service, 1968. 183 pp.

HARVEY, Chris. *Great Marques: Porsche.* London: Octopus, 1980. 96 pp.

LEFFINGWELL, Randy. *Porsche Legends.* Osceola: Motorbooks International, 1993. 228 pp.

MILLER, Susann C., and Richard F. MERRITT. *Porsche: Brochures and Sales Literature, 1948-1965.* Clifton, Virginia: M&M Publishing, 1985. 312 pp.

PORSCHE, Ferry. *Porsche Autobiographie.* Paris: Solar, n.d. 272 pp.

SEIFF, Ingo. *Porsche: Portrait of a Legend.* New York: Gallery Books, 1985. 288 pp.

SEIFFERT, Reinhard. *Carrera 4 – Porsche Allrad 1900-1990.* Munich: Südwest Verlag, 1989. 167 pp.

VIVIAN, David. *Porsche.* Paris: Solar, 1994. 70 pp.

RUMPLER

BÜSCHI, Hans, ed. *Revue Automobile – Catalogue 1983.* Bern: Hallwag, 1983, pp. 90-99.

ECKERMANN, Erick von, and C. H. BECK. *Technikgeschichte im Deutschen Museum Automobile.* Munich: C.H. Beck, n.d., p. 54.

"Rumpler Tropfen-Auto". *Automobile Quarterly,* vol. 4, no. 3 (1976), pp. 338.

TAVARD, C. H. "En avance de deux générations : les Rumpler tout-à-l'arrière étaient déjà étudiées en soufflerie". *L'Automobiliste,* no. 45 (March 1977), pp. 23-31.

SAOUTCHIK

AMENDOLA, John. "J. Saoutchik: A Selection of His Designs". *Automobile Quarterly,* vol. 9, no. 3 (1971), pp. 238-255.

VORDERMAN, Don. "Carrosserie Nonpareil". *Automobile Quarterly,* vol. 9, no. 3 (1971), pp. 236-237.

TALBOT-LAGO

RENOU, Michel. *Talbot.* Paris: EPA, 1985. Not paginated.

TATRA

DE DUBÉ, B.P.B. "Tatra: The Constant Czech". *Automobile Quarterly,* vol. 7, no. 3 (1969), pp. 302-315.

SLONIG, Jerry. "The Slippery Shapes of Paul Jaray". *Automobile Quarterly,* vol. 13, no. 3 (1976), pp. 322-335.

TOURING

ANDERLONI, Carlo F.B., and Angelo Tito ANSELMI. *Touring Superleggera: Giant among Classic Italian Coachbuilders.* Rome: Edizioni di Autocritica, 1983. 351 pp.

ANSELMI, Angelo T. "Carrozzeria Touring Superleggera". *Automobile Quarterly*, vol. 18, no. 3 (1980), pp. 296-305.

———. "Carrozzeria Touring Superleggera – Portfolio". *Automobile Quarterly*, vol. 18, no. 3 (1980), pp. 306-317.

TUCKER

BARLOW, Roger. "Escape Road: Tucker 1948". *AutoWeek*, vol. 38, no. 27 (July 4, 1988), p. 72.

COWAN, Lisa E. "Tucker: The Man, the Myth, the Movie". *Automobile Quarterly*, vol. 26, no. 3 (1988), pp. 228-233.

EGAN, Philip S. "Tremulis: The Genius behind the Tucker". *Automobile Quarterly*, vol. 26, no. 3 (1988), pp. 246-261.

———. "Tucker: Design and Destiny". *Automobile Quarterly*, vol. 26, no. 3 (1988), pp. 235-245.

———. *Design and Destiny: The Making of the Tucker Automobile*. Orange: On The Mark, 1989. 143 pp.

GAGNÉ, Luc. "Tucker, le rêveur américain". *Le Monde de l'Auto*, vol. 11, no. 3 (June/July 1993), p. 58.

LAMM, Michael. "Hoax!?". *Special Interest Autos*, December 1972/January 1973, pp. 12-19.

PEARSON, Charles T. *The Indomitable Tin Goose*. Minneapolis: Motorbooks International, 1974. 285 pp.

SPENCE, Steve. "Three Men and a Car". *AutoWeek*, vol. 38, no. 27 (July 4, 1988), pp. 22-27.

WORON, Walt. "Dreaming the Impossible Dream – The DeLorean and Its Predecessors". *Automobile Quarterly*, vol. 21, no. 2 (1988), pp. 195-196.

VOISIN

BAILEY, L. Scott. "A Visit with Gabriel Voisin". *Automobile Quarterly*, vol. 13, no. 4 (1975), pp. 340-341.

BELLU, Serge. "Des idées lumineuses". *Automobiles classiques*, no. 12 (February/March 1986), pp. 82-91.

BORGESON, Griffith. "Gabriel Voisin: Archetype of Constructors". *Automobile Quarterly*, vol. 13, no. 4 (1975), pp. 342-377.

COURTEAULT, Pierre. *Automobiles Voisin 1919-1959*. Paris: EPA, 1991. 310 pp.

LADURE, Ph. "Gabriel Voisin 1880-1973 – Feuilleton d'un chevalier en quête d'aventures". 8 pp.

SABATÈS, Fabien, and Gilles BLANCHET. *Le duel Bugatti-Voisin*. Paris: Jacques Grancher, 1982. Not paginated.

List of vehicles exhibited

1
Benz
1886
Mercedes-Benz-Museum, Stuttgart

2
La Jamais-Contente
1899
Musée national de la Voiture et du Tourisme,
Compiègne, France

2a
La Jamais-Contente
1994, replica
Lions Club International, District 103,
Île-de-France Est

3
Alfa 40/60 Ricotti
1914
Museo Storico Alfa-Romeo, Arese, Italy

4
Miller Golden Submarine
1916
Boudeman Collection, Richland, Michigan

5
Rumpler *Tropfenwagen* 0A 104
1921
Deutsches Museum, Munich

6
Voisin C6 Laboratoire
1923
Philipp Moch Collection

7
Panhard-Levassor 35 CV
1926
Musée national de l'Automobile de Mulhouse,
France, Schlumpf Collection

8
Miller 91
1928
Indianapolis Motor Speedway Hall of Fame
Museum, Indianapolis

9
Auburn 8-120 Boattail
1929
Richard Grenon, Au-Temps-Tic Auto,
Sainte-Anne-de-Bellevue, Quebec

10
Alfa-Romeo 6C 1750 *Gran Sport*
1930
Museo Storico Alfa-Romeo, Arese, Italy

11
Mercedes-Benz SSK Trossi
1932
Ralph Lauren Collection

12
Bugatti 46 coach *Profilé*
1933
Musée national de l'Automobile de Mulhouse,
France, Schlumpf Collection

13
Alfa-Romeo B *Aerodinamica*
1934
Museo Storico Alfa-Romeo, Arese, Italy

14
Chrysler Airflow CU
1934
The William F. Harrah Foundation National
Automobile Museum, Reno, Nevada

15
Voisin C25 Aérodyne
1935
Château de Vincy Collection, Switzerland

16
Lancia Astura Pinin Farina
1936
Pininfarina

17
Panhard-Levassor Dynamic 130 X76
1937
Musée Henri-Malartre, Lyon, France

18
Cord 810 Westchester
1936
The William F. Harrah Foundation National
Automobile Museum, Reno, Nevada

19
Tatra 87
1947
Walter Baran Collection, Ashland, Pennsylvania

20
Auto-Union D V12
1938
Barbara and Paul Karassik

21
Bentley 4 1/4L Embiricos
1938
Arturo Keller Collection, Petaluma, California

22
BMW 328
1938
Rosso Bianco Collection, Aschaffenburg,
Germany

PHOTOGRAPHIC CREDITS

The Montreal Museum of Fine Arts wishes to thank
the following photographers:

Jean-Paul Caron
    cat. 25, pp. 116, 118, 119
Five Valleys Photography
J. F. Gratton
    cat. 36, pp. 154, 156, 157
Eric Glanz
    cat. 7, p. 49
    cat. 12, pp. 66, 68
    cat. 27, p. 125
Martyn Goddard
    cat. 11, pp. 60, 62-63, 64
John Lamm
    cat. 31, pp. 138, 140
Phillip Mc Cordall
    cat. 20, pp. 96, 98, 99
Sophie Melcion
    cat. 6, pp. 44, 46
Photo 4
    cat. 44, pp. 186-187
Günther Raupp
    cat. 22, pp. 105, 106-107
    cat. 26, pp. 121, 122-123
    cat. 28, pp. 126, 128
    cat. 39, pp. 166, 168, 169
Olivier Staub
    Dust jacket
    cat. 14, pp. 73, 74-75
    cat. 18, pp. 89, 90-92, 93
    cat. 30, pp. 134, 135-137
    cat. 35, pp. 150-151, 152, 153
    cat. 40, pp. 170, 172-173
Guy Tessier
    cat. 9, pp. 52, 54, 55

as well as the companies, institutions and individuals who provided
the photographs illustrating this catalogue.